The Maps

This map and the one at the back of this book show the probable routes taken thousands of years ago by ancient people — wandering hunters, small nomadic groups, tribes pushed out from cultural centers, and armies. We have always supposed that man came into being in Asia. Recently, some people have come to believe that human life began in Central Africa. Nevertheless, we believe the dog became a dog somewhere in Asia, and that the most likely place is the highlands of Tibet.

Hunters used dogs to aid in gathering food. Traders carried them to trade or sell, or as gifts for potentates — and in turn took other dogs home with them. And so the dog spread over the world.

The map on the inside back cover of this book shows the "Silk Highway," the ancient route that went both east and west from Lhasa, Tibet. Silk from China was carried from Peking (now Beijing) west to Tibet, then along the mighty Indus River to the Arabian Sea. Another leg of this route followed the Ganges through India. Primitive boats crossed to Bahrain, and on to Oman. A second sea leg carried men and dogs to Egypt. Another route ran from the Tibetan Plateau southeastward to the Malay Peninsula, Sumatra, and Java, then "island hopped" from Timor to Australia's northern territories. The route running eastward from Beijing split into several lesser routes, all of which ended in Japan.

A great route westward from China went through Mongolia, skirted the Urals, followed the Volga, the Don, and the Dnepr, crossed the Caucasian Mountains and the Transcaucasus, and reached the Tigris and Euphrates in Mesopotamia.

From the Central Russian Uplands, migrating tribes traveled around, or through, the Carpathians into the Great Central Plain of Hungary, as shown on the map opposite. The Alps lay athwart the routes west. Invading armies and migrating tribes streamed through the mountain passes. Some went on to the Rhine and Germany; others turned southward into Italy; still others pressed onward through France, crossed the Pyrenees, and entered Spain. Trade routes along the Mediterranean Sea permitted trade in dogs to all of North Africa and into Spain. The British Isles were within easy reach of the European mainland by the Celts and Vikings and others from Scandinavia.

Several routes led to North and South America. From Northern Asia migrants could cross at the Bering Straits, by boat, or by land during periods when the sea level was unusually low. Once in Alaska, early people could cross North America and even reach Greenland. Others went south along the coast of Canada and the United States, moved eastward in what is now Arizona and New Mexico, then south through Mexico. Very early, boats probably left China and reached Mexico. The shortest route to South America is from the Polynesian Islands to Northern Chile and Peru. From those areas, migrants and traders could reach the Amazon basin and then travel across the continent.

Routes are shown on the maps as relatively straight lines, but were, in fact, desperately difficult. Nevertheless, both man and dog traversed the routes throughout thousands of years, so that today wherever man is, there also is the dog.

DOGS
Through
HISTORY

Maxwell Riddle

Edited by
William W. Denlinger and R. Annabel Rathman

Cover Design by
Bob Groves

DENLINGER'S PUBLISHERS, LTD.
Box 76, Fairfax, Virginia 22030

Rare sculpture of a pet dog found in
Mesopotamia. Louvre Museum, Paris.
Photo by Riddle.

Library of Congress Cataloging-in-Publication Data

Riddle, Maxwell.
    Dogs through history.

    Bibliography: p.
    Includes index.
    1. Dogs—History. I. Denlinger, William Watson. II. Rathman,
R. Annabel. III. Title.
SF422.5.R.53 1987   636.7'009   87-533
ISBN 0-87714-124-X

Acknowledgments

I have first to thank the great libraries that have helped me—the Cleveland Public Library, in particular, the John G. White Collection and the Technology Division; Hiram College Library; Kent State University Library; and Ravenna's Reed Memorial Library. Both Hiram and Ravenna used their interloan systems to locate and borrow books for me. Some books came from Ohio State, Toledo, and Youngstown State University libraries.

Japanese museums and libraries also helped to locate material. And I am particularly indebted to Junko Kimura of Tokyo for her help. Diane Anderson of Norway, and Ivan Swedrup of Stockholm, Sweden, were of invaluable aid on the Scandinavian section. Both are noted dog judges, and Mr. Swedrup, an author of many dog books, is a European titan of dogdom.

People who have given especial aid include Stanley Olsen of the University of Arizona; Dr. Barbara Lawrence, a retired anthropologist; and Qi Guo Qin, China's greatest authority on fossil dogs. They are mentioned in the text.

I have not mentioned V. W. F. Collier. Collier was an experienced Sinologist who spent many years in China. He was also an exceptional researcher and he wrote an extraordinary book called *Dogs of China and Japan in Nature and in Art.* It was published in Great Britain in the early 1920s and later in New York by Frederick A. Stokes Company, which no longer exists. The book is, of course, long out of print and extremely hard to find. But I have relied on this work, and I here pay tribute to Collier's memory.

For the most part, museums all over the world have cooperated; they are acknowledged under the pictures they provided. In some cases, restorations were needed, and I am very grateful to Dean Harris for her help with these.

Dr. Leo Mildenberg of Zurich, Switzerland, has spent many years collecting artifacts of ancient animals. Dr. Mildenberg very generously allowed me to photograph his dog artifacts while his "Ancient Animal" show was on tour. The Cleveland Museum of Art took the pictures, and Dr. Mildenberg granted me the publication rights.

Cary James was my secretary during the year in which the book was being put together. Her father, Thomas James, made the accompanying maps. Finally, I had the good fortune to have a truly great copy editor. Her grasp of the problems involved, as well as her expertise in copy editing a very technical subject are truly amazing. She is Linda Handmaker.

And finally, I had the loyal and remarkably capable help of my wife, Lenora Pentek Riddle, in proofreading the galleys.

To all I give my grateful thanks.

Maxwell Riddle

Above and below: Scandinavian stag horn carvings, Norway, 1500 A.D.

Foreword

In 1935 I began to do some research on hunting dogs. I conceived the idea of researching the origin of all dogs, but, it was not until 1939 and 1940 that I was able to devote any time to it. I was a reporter on the *Cleveland Press*. And about that time I was assigned to cover the federal courts and federal agencies. Most of them took long lunch hours, which enabled me to spend my own lunch hours at Cleveland's magnificently endowed Main Public Library.

The library housed the great John G. White collection of very rare books. In those days, it was not locked up, so day after day I was able to browse and study. Even after the collection was put under lock and key, I was allowed to study the volumes I needed.

I soon discovered that the origins of dogs cannot be traced without studying the history of ancient man. I was chiefly interested in the dogs of the Americas and quickly realized that I would have to learn Spanish, not only modern Spanish, but antique Spanish—the Spanish of the conquistadors and discoverers. And so I took a course at the Berlitz School of Languages, then checked with Spain.

But the problem existed for other languages, too. Homer wrote of the "wine dark sea." What color is a wine dark sea? What color did Homer actually mean? Had our own color vision changed over the millenia? In Spain, and in other countries, terms for colors were different from those we use today.

I think many readers will find many surprises in the book, since I, too, was surprised—by the story of Nero as a strikebreaker in ancient Rome, by the discovery of Jomon pottery in Peru, dating to several thousand years before the Peruvians themselves had learned how to make pottery.

This book is not an exhaustive text. Rather it is designed to make excellent reading while shedding light on the world of the past. It is designed to show that highly intelligent people and their dogs wandered the world long before the beginning of recorded history.

M. R.

ANOLFINI MARRIAGE, painted by Jan Van Eyck, ca. 1422. Note the small dog of Cairn Terrier type. Courtesy, National Gallery, London.

6

Contents

Pre-Christian rock engravings. Scandinavia.

Hundreds of rock engravings, such as this one, have been found from Scandinavia to Spain. About 1500 B.C.

8

1.   *Early Ancestors of the Dog*

A world-famous anthropologist once remarked that, in tracing the origin of man, nothing anyone could say would be free of challenge. So it is with the dog. In a very general way, we are able to trace its history through nearly sixty million years. But we do not know with any certainty the direct ancestor of the dog nor the time when the first true dogs appeared on earth.

The canid family (*Canidae*) can be traced back sixty million years to the creodonts. It was a time when placental mammals were developing. The creodonts were carnivorous animals having incisors with closed roots, a distinct fibula or calf bone, and certain improvements in the inner ear.

A descendant of Creodonta was Miacis, a civetlike animal that gave way to the increasingly doglike Cynodictis and Daphaenus, the ancestor of the bear. Cynodictis ran on its toes, as do modern dogs; Daphaenus walked on its heels, as do modern bears. From Cynodictis came an improved form, Cynodesmus. And from Cynodesmus came Tomarctus.

This did not happen within a few generations. The long evolutionary process required approximately thirty million years. Tomarctus, along with some extinct relatives—Borophagus, Hyaenodon, and Hyaenognathus—all developed in North America.

The puzzle begins here. Tomarctus, or its descendants, disappeared from North America. We cannot even guess why. And although we know that wolves, domesticated dogs, foxes, and fennecs descended from Tomarctus, we do not know how, nor even when.

The ancestors of the horse developed similarly in North America. They, too, suddenly disappeared from the continent. Despite this fact, the American Museum of Natural History in New York has an exhibit of the entire skeletal development of the horse. But no such skeletal line has ever been fully developed for the origins of the dog.

In his *Living Mammals of the World*, Ivan T. Sanderson has this to say:

Thus we come to a very strange impasse, to wit: are all domestic dogs merely altered forms of the wolf, or are they descendants of some animal that is now totally extinct? If the latter, where are the fossilized bones of that animal? A third alternative is that our domestic dogs may have been developed from different strains of wolves, jackals, and other extinct animals at different times and in different places.

To resolve these questions, researchers have been crossing dogs, wolves, and dingoes for one hundred years or more. Others have made studies of skulls, teeth, leg bones, and feet. Still others have tried to solve the puzzle based on patterns of behavior. But the answers remain elusive.

In their book *Pleistocene Mammals of North America*, Bjorn Kurtén and Elaine Anderson point out that the canids arose during the Oligocene epoch and reached an astonishing diversity during the Miocene.

It is perhaps more understandable if we simplify this by stating that the Oligocene, Miocene, and Pliocene were successive epochs during the Tertiary period when the Cascade Range was being formed in western North America. The next epoch was the Pleistocene, which was one of glaciation—the Ice Age. During this epoch, many mammals developed into greater size, leading to the descriptive term, age of giantism.

Sanderson's third suggestion, that wolves, jackals, and extinct forms may all have been in the ancestry of the dog, might fit into the great diversity of forms mentioned by Kurtén and Anderson.

Sanderson's question concerning the fossilized bones of the extinct canid that might have preceded the dog is not particularly germane. For one thing, insofar as fossils are concerned, much of Asia remains unexplored. Moreover, there are "missing links" in the fossil records of most animals, including man. Scientists, searching for transitional forms in many species, have been continuously frustrated.

Dr. William G. Haag suggested in 1948 that the direct ancestor of the dog was an unknown and now extinct canid in the Pleistocene epoch. As noted earlier, during this time of glaciation over much of the world, many small mammals moved toward giantism for their species. Haag further guessed that, whatever the age in which this small mutant canid developed, the domestication of its descendant, the dog, might have occurred between 12,000 and 13,500 B.C.

Darwin's theory of evolution postulates that occasional mutations toward a superior being occurred over immense periods of time, even over epochs. But today many scientists—anatomists, evolutionary geneticists, and paleontologists—suggest another form of evolution. A group of mutations, a random leap or jump, may come all at once to make a vastly superior organism. This does not negate Darwinism, but merely adds to it.

This might answer Sanderson's question on the whereabouts of fossil bones of the dog's ancestry. The answer would be, there are none. There may have been no transitional forms, just a sudden leaping over and beyond them.

Richard and Alice Fiennes, distinguished zoologists and anatomists, have collaborated in producing two important books on the subject—*The Order of Wolves* and *The Natural History of Dogs*. Their opinion is that all breeds of dog can be traced to several varieties of wolf, living and extinct. Their anatomical analyses are brilliant.

But it seems that the argument fails on one particular point. The domestic dog probably surpasses all other animals, wild or domestic, in the plasticity of its germ plasm. This has made possible the astounding variation in dog breeds, from Chihuahua to Saint Bernard, for instance. Wolves, on the other hand, do not demonstrate this plasticity. Many varieties are so similar only dedicated scientists with years of experience can distinguish the difference. Sometimes even they disagree on the varieties. Yet no one has any problem recognizing that a Miniature Pinscher is not an Afghan Hound. (Reasons for believing the dog is not just a domestic wolf will be given in another chapter.)

Thus, while Richard and Alice Fiennes have brilliantly developed their point of view, it is as subject to challenge as any other theory, including my own. However, as will be seen later, their work is immensely valuable in another respect.

Now comes the question, when did the animal we know as the dog actually become a dog? Again we can only theorize. It often is said that all the domestic animals and plants known today were domesticated before recorded history began. This seems to be true in most particulars, even though scientists keep pushing that date farther and farther into the mists of what once was.

Exceptions are sometimes made in the cases of the turkey and the Australian shell parakeet, or budgerigar. Both appear to be still in the process of domestication. Thus, the turkey has been reintroduced into the wild and it thrives, even though hunters kill many thousands annually. And I have watched budgies that have survived in the wild, even in a northern Ohio winter.

A good place to start speculation on the dog's actual origin is the Pleistocene epoch, the great Ice Age. As Kurtén and Anderson pointed out, mammals underwent an astonishing diversity of type during this period. However, the only clues truly available deal with the discovery of domestic dogs, not with their undomesticated ancestors. The earliest evidences are a fossil jaw and teeth found in a shallow cave at an archaeological site known as Pelagawra, near the town of Kirkuk in Iraq. They were found by Dr. Bruce Lowe during an expedition directed by Dr. Robert Braidwood of the Oriental Institute at the University of Chicago. The British Museum fluorene-dated the fossil at 14,000 years ago. Two of the world's greatest authorities—Dr. Barbara Lawrence, then of Harvard, and Dr. Stanley Olsen of the University of Arizona—studied the find and proved that the animal was a true dog. And it was associated with man. That is, human remains were found at the same time level.

Dr. Lawrence discovered another fossil dog in the Jaguar Cave of the Birch Creek Valley, Lemhi County, Idaho. This was carbon dated at from 9500 to 8400 B.C. and therefore is possibly 11,500 years old. Again the fossil was found to be associated with relics of man. Another fossil, this one from Turkey, was carbon dated at about 7000 B.C.

Dr. Lawrence concluded that the typically domestic dog characters of these fossils indicated that domestication must have taken place much earlier to allow for the appearances of characters that are essentially those of modern dogs. These characters, as distinguished from those of the wolf, will be discussed in the next chapter.

If one follows Darwin's theory of occasional favorable mutations occurring over immensely long periods of time, then the Pleistocene epoch might certainly be the time when the dog gradually developed. Even if one follows the new addition to Darwin, that in some cases a group of favorable mutations might occur almost simultaneously, there still must have been a long period before the dog actually became associated with people. In that case, the late Pleistocene may have been the starting point.

In brief, this summarizes what is known and what is speculated about the origin of the dog. The next chapter will consider its domestication.

2. *Domestication of the Dog*

If we are not certain about when a dog became a true dog, or how, neither are we certain about when it became a domestic animal. Nor do we know who domesticated it, or how. There are many theories: some seem to be convenient rationalizations; all, including my own, are subject to challenge. It may be that a complex of factors involving parts from all the theories made domestication possible.

First, what is meant by the terms domestic and tame? Webster's has several definitions of domestic, including "peculiar to or affecting the intimate relations and amenities of a family group living together," and "living near or about the habitations of man." Tame is defined, "made tractable and useful to man."

All three definitions can apply to the dog. In fact, Webster's also says "domestic—tame." Yet the meanings of the two words are vastly different when applied to most animals.

For instance, Webster's second definition of domestic applies to the rat, as the dictionary also states. Rats have cast in their lot with that of man, and all the centuries of trapping and poisoning have not changed them. They are highly intelligent and gentle, and they would make great pets except for one problem. As with some other rodents, their teeth continue to grow. So rats must gnaw constantly to keep them worn down; otherwise, their teeth would grow to the point that they could no longer open their mouths, and they consequently would starve.

On the other hand, an elephant can be tamed and made to fit Webster's definition, "made tractable and useful to man." But it cannot be domesticated. Wild elephants are caught and trained. They fear man and obey him. But elephants born in captivity do not have the same degree of fear of man and consequently are dangerous, as any animal trainer or zookeeper can attest. The import of this is that a wild animal is always a wild animal. Capture and tame two of them, then breed them—the offspring are still wild.

13

Two animals' histories bear comparison with that of the rat. The first is the horse. Horses formed a major item of diet for primitive men. Apparently horses were rounded up and then driven and stampeded over cliffs to their deaths. How strange that, having been terrorized and slaughtered for so many centuries, horses still became domestic animals, still cast in their lot with that of man.

The second concerns the Euranan reindeer. People in northern Siberia apparently used domestic reindeer at least 2,500 years ago. They are alluded to in Chinese writings as early as 500 B.C. This would indicate that they had been domesticated much earlier.

The reindeer is one of the most remarkable of all living creatures. Herds of them live in a half-wild state. They do not need stables to protect them from Arctic storms, nor do they need to be fenced. They are self-supporting, living chiefly on a lichen known as reindeer moss. Their meat is delicious; their milk, one of the richest in the entire animal kingdom. Their sinews make immensely tough thread; their hides make warm clothes.

When needed, the reindeer can be rounded up. The Lapps use them to haul sledges because their feet are ideal for going through snow, slush, or mud. In Siberia they can be ridden. They can pull astonishing loads, and some evidence suggests they were used for drafts before other people used the dog.

It seems to me a miracle that, being subject to slaughter and hard work and being allowed to roam free, the reindeer still remains a domestic animal.

In light of the paradoxes of domestic and tame, what are some of the theories on the domestication of the dog? One theory holds that primitive hunters brought wolf puppies to their camps to delight the children. The pups grew up tame, and, being predators, joined the hunt with enthusiasm. They were rewarded with a share of the meat.

Another theory contends that primitive hunters, far from their camps, were lonely and fearful. They captured wolf puppies, raised them carefully, then took them along for companionship as well as for aid in hunting. Still another postulates that the wolf puppies, having grown, could be slaughtered for food during times of hunger. Moreover, their pelts could be made into warm clothing. Modern Eskimos still feel that a parka trimmed with wolf is the ultimate in fashion.

Supporting the food theory is the fact that dogs are still eaten by people in various parts of the world. In Newfoundland during the years 1794 and 1795, Aaron Thomas reported in his diary that the hams of a Newfoundland dog, properly prepared, were superior to the celebrated "Hams of Bayonne" in Gascony.

Another domestication theory is that hunger drove wolves to hang around the camps of men and scavenge for leavings. The wolves gradually became tame and began to take part in the hunts. This scavenger theory has been cited in descriptions of primitive camps in the South Seas islands. Those camps or villages that had dogs were reasonably clear of flies and stench. The villages with no dogs eventually had to be abandoned because the flies and stench became unbearable.

There can be a grisly twist to the scavenger theory. Early men did not bury their dead until they gained the concept of an afterlife. Before that, bodies were tossed out of the camps or were left where they fell in the forests. So the tamed wolves, become dogs, feasted upon them.

In Biblical times, half-wild, homeless, and hungry dogs probably scavenged outside the walled towns. In 2 Kings 9:36, we read, the "word of the Lord, which he spoke by his servant, Elijah the Tishbite. In the territory of Jezreel the dogs shall eat the flesh of Jezebel, and the corpse of Jezebel shall be as dung upon the face of the field . . . ."

Even today in Tibet the bodies of the dead are chopped up by special butchers and fed to vultures and pariah dogs. And in some areas of Alaska, wolves, polar bears, and probably dogs once fed on bodies that could not be buried.

One more theory is that man found the wolf a useful guardian of the campsite, perhaps an ancient cave. It is in such caves that the earliest fossils of true domestic dogs have been found.

As I have mentioned, all these theories are subject to serious challenge. Consider first the theory that the dog is merely a tamed wolf. A wolf can be tamed, but that does not make it a domestic animal. If two wolves are bred together, the offspring will be wild animals still.

A change from wild-tame to domestic-tame may have occurred gradually over many generations. But it seems unlikely that primitive men, with their wandering lifestyle, would carry forward such a continuity. And I think the change would have to come either over epochs of continuity or by a sudden genetic leap in mentality.

Richard and Alice Fiennes write of wolves hanging around the camps of North American explorers, the explorers tying out their bitches to be bred to these wolves. The Fiennes also claim that the Eskimos have always done likewise.

Yet history is full of accounts of mortal enmity between wolves and dogs, wolves destroying entire dog teams. Two Alaskan trappers, Black Luk and Black Beaver of Noatak, came upon a wolf killing a bitch with nursing pups. One pup that they saved, known as Goldfang, became one of the most famous of Alaskan sled dogs. A modern account of wolves killing an entire dog sled team can be found in Robert Specht's story of an Alaskan school teacher, Tisha. And the fear of dogs for even a bitch wolf which was raised from puppyhood with them can be found in Nancy Russell's account in my own book, *The Wild Dogs in Life and Legend*.

In analyzing the accounts of explorers that wolves hung around their camps at night and that bitches were tied out to mate with them, one must know something of the early history of North America.

The Spaniards brought with them huge numbers of horses and dogs, many of which escaped and ran wild. Eager for gold, the Spaniards also secretly bartered away their dogs and horses. Many of these escaped from the Indians and ran wild. But also, poverty and lack of food in some of the Indian tribes forced many of the dogs to live in the wild in order to survive.

Spanish, English, or American, the early explorers were not necessarily experts on animals. They called the shadowy animals that lurked beyond the light of their campfires and howled, wolves. But they were almost certainly feral dogs—dogs gone wild. Of course, the bitches of the camp would recognize that they were dogs.

Before the snowmobile began to replace the use of dogs in the far north, I questioned many Eskimo drivers about dog-wolf crosses. They denied making them. First, there was the mortal enmity, then the fact that the sled dogs sometimes had to be tied on six-foot chains for days or a week or more at a time. Wolves, the Eskimos said, were far too nervous to stand that. So if crosses were made, they were seldom successful.

Another problem of the theory of the dog-wolf crosses is that male wolves seldom reach sexual maturity before age three; females, two. The evidence indicates that other adults never reach that point. This avoids dominance fights which might destroy the pack. Instead, the "aunts and uncles" remain infertile and help to take care of the pups. This severely cuts down the possibility of wolf-dog crosses except by the force of unusual circumstances. Also, pack size would be better maintained since only one litter of pups would be whelped each year. One ancient Eskimo, who denied such crosses were ever made, said "We tell it to the people (outside the Arctic). That is what they want to hear, and it sounds good."

Consider the theory that man may have domesticated the dog, not only as a hunter, but as a source of food during the winter or during other periods of near starvation. If so, why did he not follow the example of those who domesticated the reindeer? Moreover, why did he not choose a more likely candidate such as the bear? It grows to huge size as compared to a dog or wolf. It sleeps all winter, so it does not have to be fed. Its meat is excellent food and its hide would make far warmer clothes and blankets than could be made from a dog or wolf hide. Buried in our psyche is an ancient feeling of happiness and security furnished by lying on a bearskin rug in front of a log fire. It is as though our cells remember a time when our ancestors lay on such rugs, with a fire at the cave's mouth to keep out the cold and predators.

Bears could have pulled far heavier sledge loads than dogs and might even have been taught to pull a plow. If primitive hunters brought home wolf puppies, so, too, they must have brought bear cubs to their camps. Even today, hunters shoot bear mothers and bring home cubs. But half- to full-grown bears, supposedly tame, are safe only when muzzled. Neither in the past nor today have they become domesticated. Why? I think it is because they have refused to be.

As for the campsite guardian theory, primitive people probably did not see wolves as possible watchdogs because wolves don't bark. And primitive people, who knew far more about the world around them than we can ever know, would have noted that fact.

A respected authority on canine behavior once remarked to me, "You practical dog men see a side of dogs that we never see in the laboratory." Perhaps that gives me the right to suggest my own theory.

I believe the dog made the first move toward domestication. It seems to me that at some point, long before the Pelagawra fossil, a great mutation occurred in the mentality of a canid. It would have been a mutant canid, a cousin to the wolf, neither wolf nor dog. Yet the mental mutation caused the animal to cast in its lot with that of man.

The urge, while strong, would have been tentative at first, tempered by uncertainty and some fear. But primitive men, so alert to every facet of animal life, would have recognized the urge. Their own moves would have been tentative at first. Then, as hesitation changed to understanding, they would have proceeded to cement the bond. The process would be long and slow, and it would embody certain physical changes that would enable people like Dr. Barbara Lawrence and Stanley Olsen to distinguish dog fossil from wolf fossil.

The great Ice Age was ending. Men and animals had been forced to make radical adjustments to the ice. Now more adjustments were needed. The process would be slow for all creatures. Those which could not adjust would perish. Some would change but would remain completely wild. Others—those which Edwin Colbert of the American Museum of Natural History called "sociable animals"—would make tentative approaches to people. Carbon dating of once living materials is the surest method of determining the approximate age of a fossil.

Using this method, the Pelagawra dog lived 14,000 years ago. The Jaguar dog whose remains were found in an American cave, lived 10,000 years ago. Thus, dogs which lived as far apart as Iraq and northern United States are the oldest dog fossils ever found. And they are older than any other domestic animal. Carbon dating gives 9000 B.C. for sheep, 6500 B.C. for goats, and 6000 B.C. for cattle and pigs. These dates prove that the dog was the first domestic animal.

How do scientists identify a jawbone and some teeth, or a part of a cranium, as belonging to a dog and not a wolf? The dog's teeth are smaller and closer together. The brain case is as much as 25% smaller. Both the leg bones and feet are lighter and smaller. The jaw is usually shorter and broader.

The compaction of the teeth and the shortening of the jaw are considered evidence of domestication. The theory is that when the dog became domesticated, it had to give up a perfect diet for the inferior one furnished by people. The differences in very young puppies might not be great. This can account for the very bitter arguments as to whether the so-called Star Carr dog of Yorkshire was a dog or a wolf.

Still, with the possible exception of very young animals, the differences between dogs and wolves, even fossil dogs and wolves, are sufficient to make positive identifications. One major difference, which could not be determined by the study of fossil animals, concerns sweating. Every person who has owned a sled dog in the north, or a hunting dog in snow country, knows that the dog's feet pick up snowballs. These form on the pads and between the toes. The snow freezes onto the sweat which issues from the feet. But wolves do not have sweat glands in their feet.

Three researchers, Michael W. Sands, Raymond P. Coppinger, and Carleton J. Phillips, noted this fact. Dr. Coppinger is a respected sled dog racer. He observed that snowballs do not form on the feet of wolves, at least North American wolves. The three researchers investigated. They tested twelve wolves, six from the Boston Zoo and six caught as pups at the Naval Arctic Research Laboratory. The test dogs were Siberian Huskies, animals that have been used by the Eskimos for a thousand dog generations. As expected, all the dogs tested showed spontaneous sweating. The wolves did not. Under anesthesia, the wolves' footpads were thermally stimulated almost to the point of burning. Sweating could not be induced. The lack of sweating response was identical in both sets of wolves.

If dogs were merely tamed wolves, it might be expected that they would lack sweat glands in their foot pads. Moreover, since the Eskimos depended upon dogs for their lives, they would have bred for this quality. And this would be so even if their modern sled dogs were crosses between wolves and dogs. All the evidence, therefore, seems indisputable to me that the dog developed individually from some as yet unknown canid offshoot of the ancestor of the wolves.

Footprint of a dog which walked across this brick as it lay drying in the sun when it was being made at Ur, Iraq, about 2100 B.C. The brick is stamped with an inscription which tells that "Ur-Nammu, the King of Ur, has built his temple for Nanna, his Lord. . . ." Courtesy University of Pennsylvania Museum.

19

Mosaic hunting scene by Gnossis, earliest known signed mosaic, about 600 B.C.
Courtesy of Archaeological Museum of Thessalonike. Early Greek stage hunters
proved courage by going naked as did the Elamite wild boar hunters.

20

3.   *The Great Families of Dogs*

The Glacial or Pleistocene epoch, which we tend to call the Ice Age, lasted about one million years. Actually, four intervals of maximum glaciation alternated with intervals of warming. During the warming periods, glaciers would begin to melt and recede towards the poles.

During periods of heavy glaciation, water levels in seas and lakes would be low. Land bridges would form, as at the Bering Strait between Alaska and Asia and in the Torres Strait between New Guinea and Australia. These bridges allowed animals and man to migrate over land. When the glaciers melted, the land bridges would be under water. North America would be cut off from Asia, and Australia from New Guinea, unless the straits were crossed by boat.

At roughly 60,000 years ago, the Glacial epoch lost its grip over the temperate zone and subtropical lands. As the glaciers receded, flora and fauna began to occupy the freed lands. Great northern forests grew where ice had been, and flora of other types covered lands the forest had not. In the far north, where forests could not grow, lichens covered the earth to supply food for reindeer and other animals, large and small.

Since, as pointed out earlier, the end of the Ice Age brought an astonishing increase in the size and variation of mammals, it is possible that the dog made its appearance at this time. This would not be the domestic dog, since domestication might still have required a very long time. But it might mark dogs' very early moves toward domestication. They would have begun their own migrations around the world, and the migrations might have followed those of primitive men. Those men, observant of every form of wildlife, would have recognized the tentative moves of the animals and would have responded in kind.

Since the Pelagawra dog was a truly domesticated species by 14,000 years ago, it is possible that it had taken as long as 40,000 years for domestication to be completed. Yet, in another sense, the dog still had a long way to go. The Pelagawra was probably a hunting dog, but not until the domestication of other animals could the dog fulfill its destiny. And, as shown earlier, the other domestic animals came much later.

There is a theory on the radiation of human cultures that goes something like this: Cultural centers were formed that at first were small. They then began to widen. Great changes occurred in these centers, and those people on the outskirts who were unable or unwilling to change were pushed outward.

According to this theory, people would have migrated to the Arctic, to the southern tip of South America, to Australia and Tasmania, to the jungles of Africa, and on to Africa's southern tip. These great, world-wide migrations might have begun at the close of the Ice Age and would have lasted for many thousands of years. And dogs, whether fully or partially domesticated, would have gone with men.

Richard and Alice Fiennes believe there are four great families of dogs. They may be right in supposing that these have developed from four families of wolves. But it is also possible, and I think more likely, that over the long period of 40,000 years these families developed simply by adapting to their environment. While it is myth to suppose any pure strain of dogs goes back to the end of the Ice Age, certain characteristics have remained to indicate the families.

As the age of giantism began for the mammals, one group of dogs appears to have grown toward giant size and to have moved into the Himalayas and other mountainous areas of Asia. This group, aside from its giant size, is characterized by a deep "stop." The stop is the "step up" that divides the skull from the nasal passages and muzzle. In these dogs, two large air chambers or sinuses are separated by a small bone.

Some anatomists suggest that the function of these chambers is to warm air before it reaches the lungs. The air is further warmed in the lungs and thus helps to warm the chambers when it is expired. Others believe that these air chambers only fill with air as it is expired. Sinuses also are situated in the maxillary bone. They seem to help widen the skull, which permits mightier jaws—an advantage for mountain dogs that might have to attack large animals.

To this group—dogs with deep stops—belong the *Mastiff* type dogs, the mountain dogs such as the Great Pyrenees, the Saint Bernard, and others, and all of the sporting breeds. They all have fold-over ears, or drop ears as they are sometimes called. Some writers have suggested that the deep stop and large sinuses give these dogs greater scenting powers.

However, the air chambers have no nerve endings that could send scent messages to the brain.

A second family of dogs can be said to belong to the *Spitz* group, or *northern* dogs. To this family belong all of the sled dogs, most of the shepherd dogs, and the terriers. Most of the Japanese breeds, such as the Akita, also belong to this group. The northern dogs—sometimes called Northern Forest dogs—have moderate stops, erect ears, and generally curled tails. Efforts to change the tails to the type that waves above the body when it moves have been made with the Siberian Husky and the Alaskan Malamute.

The shepherd dogs may have erect or drop ears and tails with brushes that hang down with only a slight curve at the end. The normal stop of the family has been altered by selective breeding to be almost nonexistent in such breeds as the Collie and Shetland Sheepdog.

The terriers are so much a British Isles development that the British are unwilling to recognize any breed as a terrier that does not come from Britain or that does not descend from British stock. These dogs are descended from the northern family, but the stop has been virtually eliminated by selective breeding. However, it is still difficult to keep the ears folded and the tails from curling.

A third group, which can be called *coursing or cursorial hounds,* were called Gaze Hounds by the Romans. They are of the Greyhound type, built to pursue desert game or to course over rough, open country with few trees. Since, for the most part, they are desert or warm-climate dogs, the stop has been virtually eliminated. The dogs have no need to warm the air entering the lungs.

The fourth family includes the *primitive* dogs. They probably accompanied primitive people who were forced to move away from the cultural centers. It may have been 50,000 years ago that unknown people took the Dingo to Australia. Then, finding the section nearest Asia inhospitable, they returned to Asia, leaving some Dingoes behind. These dogs then spread rapidly over the continent.

The primitive group includes, besides the Dingo, the Telomian of Malaysia, the Basenji of central Africa, the Sinhala Hound of Sri Lanka, the Thai Dog of Thailand, and the pariahs, including the Canaan Dog of Israel.

Some dogs, such as the Doberman Pinscher, might be placed in one of several groups. The toy dogs, too, are a mixture that defies classification, except for the Pomeranian, which is a northern dog.

Until quite recently, the spread of both dogs and people around the world had remained a puzzle. It is true that Chinese artifacts had been found in Mesopotamia. But it remained for the famed Scandinavian explorer, Thor Heyerdahl, to prove that world-wide commerce was possible. Heyerdahl built a reed boat which he sailed across the Pacific. Later, he used a reed boat in sailing from Asia across the Arabian Sea to show that ancient people could, and certainly did, sail from Mohenjo Daro to Mesopotamia.

By 3000 B.C. the four great families of dogs were well established. Examples of all families probably could be found world wide as early as 3000 B.C., and certainly by Greek and Roman times. The rise of the great Mesopotamian civilizations made documentation of the history of dogs possible during their time of glory.

From Catal Huyuk. Earliest known painting of a dog. Man shoots arrow and dog assists in chase. Reconstructed by Dean Harris, as shown here.

4.   *The Stone Age Dogs*

People in the Western World who try to unravel the past take it for granted that civilization began in Mesopotamia. Our culture is based upon that of the vanished cities of Mesopotamia, North Africa, Greece, Rome, Phoenicia, and other countries. But there are many terms which must be defined. What is meant, for instance, by the term civilization. For historians and archaeologists, it means a culture based on agriculture, and established cities with permanent homes, domesticated animals, etc. Such a culture has the time to develop crafts, art, literature, and a written language.

Ancient Mesopotamia seems to offer perfect examples of vanished civilizations. The area is dotted by tells. A tell is the ruin of a dead city. In ancient times, a conquering army might destroy a city, reducing it almost to rubble. But a new city would be built over the ruins of the older one. And this might happen half a dozen times. Finally the site would be abandoned forever. Then the sands of the desert would gradually cover the ruins, leaving a mound or tell.

A tell thus offered the promise of great reward to archaeologists. The top layer, that is the last civilization, would have various finely dressed tools, clay tablets of writing, often history of the city, examples of sculptures, pottery, etc. And sometimes, also, literature, either prose or poetry. As each dig or excavation proceeded downward, poorer craftsmanship would be found. Evidences of pottery would disappear, and this would indicate a "preceramic" level. Dating was often difficult, and depended in part upon comparisons with other cultures, historic records of dynasties, etc. However, the coming of the atomic age gave archaeologists a new and more accurate dating tool. It is called the carbon-14 test and it measures the extent of decay or radioactive carbon in wood, charcoal, bones, and other organic materials.

Archaeologists have always been on the lookout for evidences of domestic animals. The fossil remains of their bones would indicate the degree of civilization at the time the animals lived. Thus, in excavating the layers in the Pelagawra Cave, the fossil remains of a dog were found, and at the same level with the artifacts of ancient men. Thus, it is said, the dog was associated with man.

It is assumed that it took an immense amount of time to transform people of a hunter-gatherer culture, and their necessarily nomadic life, into sedentary farmers and breeders of domestic animals. The tells of Mesopotamia gave no indication of this. Dr. Robert Braidwood of the University of Chicago began to try to answer that puzzle. Dr. Braidwood reasoned that the transformation might have occurred in the highlands and slopes of the Zagros Mountains of Kurdistan in Iraq. There were small tells there. They had been ignored by earlier diggers since they offered fewer opportunities for spectacular finds. Braidwood, himself, had difficulty in convincing his own sponsors that he should excavate there. Braidwood also reasoned that the area had once abounded in "domesticable or domesticated" animals—dogs, sheep, goats, pigs, and possibly horses.

Braidwood and his wife, Linda, began their dig at a three and a half acre tell known as Jarmo. They stripped away various layers of occupation until they reached the lowest one. They found the bones of many animals, domestic or not. But there was no evidence of pottery. Still, Jarmo is important in the history of the dog because the Braidwoods found a miniature unfired clay figurine of a dog. It appears to have been sculpted using a living dog as a model. We cannot guess the size of the living dog nor its purpose—pet, hunter, shepherd, guard dog.

The figurine is a charming thing. The dog looks as if it might have been related to the Lhasa Apso or, if very large, a shaggy coated sheepdog. That some artist, at that stage in history, could have carved such a likeness of a dog is a miracle almost beyond belief. Of course, it is possible that the figurine was lost by some stranger to the site. Even so, it is a miracle that it could have survived some ninety centuries. Finally, it is a tribute to the Braidwoods, and to all archaeologists, for the detail and care of the dig that enabled someone to find it.

Jarmo also yielded carbonized forms of three kinds of wheat, emmer, and peas. There were farming tools, mortars and pestles for grinding grain, sickles, etc. There were stone axes with finely ground cutting edges, and equipment used in weaving. Most of the animal bones were of cattle, sheep, goats, and dogs, though proof that they were domesticated is lacking. Jarmo can be dated at 7000 B.C., and at the time the Braidwoods excavated, it was the oldest farming community then known.

However, Jarmo's claim to being the first farming community did not last long. From the early 1900s on, Jericho had known excavators. Among these was Professor Dorothy Garrod in 1930. Some twenty years later, Kathleen Kenyon began her "dig." From 1952 to 1958, she excavated the mound at Jericho. She dug deeply and carefully into the Tell-es-Sultan, a ruin seventy feet high, covering ten acres. The tell was part of the oasis of Jericho.

The Biblical saying "going down to Jericho" is quite literally true. Jericho is at the northern end of the Dead Sea, and it lies 825 feet below sea level, thus making it one of the driest areas in the world. Yet it has a marvelous spring which has watered a remarkable oasis. Wandering groups visited it and camped there repeatedly over many centuries. They may have visited Jericho as early as 7800 B.C. But eventually one group decided to make Jericho their permanent home. They certainly had to defend themselves against warring groups which wanted to take over the area themselves.

Dr. Kenyon dug deep into the Tell-es-Sultan, and came upon a massive wall, thirteen feet high. Inside the wall was a stone tower of excellent masonry, twenty-six feet high. It has an internal stairway leading up to the battlements. Yes, Jericho had a wall some 6000 years before Joshua is said to have blown it down.

Jericho's earliest inhabitants practiced a primitive type of agriculture. The lack of evidence of herded animals suggests that the earliest inhabitants may have depended partly upon hunting for meat. Jericho was separated from Mesopotamia by the vast Syrian Desert, so herds of wild animals must have visited the oasis for water.

But Jericho did have dogs. The fossil remains of two dogs have been discovered. One was a large dog, the other much smaller. If Jericho had no herded animals, it had no need for shepherd dogs. But it almost certainly had need of guard dogs to warn of the approach of nomadic groups. And it is likely that it had dogs for the chase. We probably are not far amiss in suggesting that Jericho did have primitive dogs of coursing type, plus smaller dogs that might help to catch wild game.

The discoveries of the Braidwoods and Dr. Kenyon stimulated digs in other areas of the Near East. And suddenly it became obvious that

Jericho and Jarmo were not alone in changing from a hunter-gatherer culture to one of agriculture. The latter would permit the establishment of great cities with a high level of cultural achievement. It seemed that nomads everywhere were taking the first halting steps forward. Hundreds of years, or perhaps a thousand, would be required for the change. And in the meantime, those who refused to give up the old ways, who refused to exchange the spear for the hoe, were driven farther and farther from the cultural centers and into the unknown lands beyond.

The position of the dog was still shadowy. Archaeologists continued to ask the same questions. Was the dog a hunting companion, a cave or house guardian, a pet, a herder of domestic animals, or a scavenger that cleaned up the garbage around the camp sites and villages.

At least part of the answer came from southern Turkey when a tell called Catal Hüyük, a riverside town on the Konya Plain, was uncovered. It had had enough houses to support a population of 5,000 people, and it must have existed for a thousand years or more. It had passed from human memory for nearly seven millenia. However, as of now, Catal Huyuk is the oldest town yet discovered. It had flourished about 9,000 years ago.

The people of Catal Huyuk were farmers, shepherds, and traders. They lived along an ancient trade route. Traders from distant places would bring calcite, alabaster, gems, and other goods. The people of Catal Hüyük had learned to smelt copper. This they could use for barter, along with grain, wool, and hides. The people lived in houses that had no doors. Entrance was made through holes either well up the sides of rounded walls, or in the roof. In her 1976 documentary called The People of Kau, Leni Riefenstahl showed a southern Sudan tribe that still builds and lives in that type of house. However, the people of Catal Hüyük sometimes had multi-roomed houses, and even shrine rooms or shrine houses.

Some of the shrines contained the heads of bulls—clay modelled over the actual skulls. The bulls were an obvious symbol of power. And as if the artists were showing their work to all the later centuries, as well as to the bulls, some wall paintings showed men kissing the noses of bulls.

These people believed in an afterlife. The bodies of the dead were exposed outside the village so that vultures and jackals could tear away the flesh of the corpses. The skeletons then were buried under the homes, often with gifts. (As will be shown later, the custom of exposing the bodies still exists in Tibet.)

The people of Çatal Hüyük engaged in hunting. Whether they did so as a means of augmenting their food supply, or simply for recreation, is not known. One artist painted a very primitive hunting scene upon the wall of a house. It depicts a hunter loosing an arrow at a gazelle or stag, and a dog has joined the hunt. It is our earliest sure proof that dogs were already used for hunting. And it marks a milestone in the history of the dog, for it is our earliest picture of a dog.

The painting resembles the work of a child in its use of matchstick-like characters. The dog has a very long body which sits on four sticks for legs. But crude as the painting is, and practically obliterated by time as it is, there is no question as to the identities of the hunter, the hunted, and the dog. And since the painting is a true coursing scene, one can speculate that the dog has the relatively long body of a true coursing dog, however primitive it may have been.

Thus far, in tracing the history of man and his animals, the dog has remained in the shadows. Strangely, he emerges in a culture about which very little is known. Until quite recently we knew about the Elamites mainly from a scant Biblical reference, and from a comment by the Greek geographer Strabo. We quote here from both sources.

They shall fall amid those who are slain by the sword, and with her shall lie all her multitudes . . . . Assyria is there, and all her company . . . . Elam is there, and all her multitude about her grave; all of them slain, fallen by the sword, . . . who spread terror in the land of the living . . . . (Ezek. 32:20-24)

And from Strabo: "Parts of the Plain of Elam are so hot that if a snake tried to cross the road at midday, it would be fried before it could reach the other side."

Elam can be dated roughly as having flourished for 2,000 years from about 5,000 years ago until about 3,000 years ago. It was far enough advanced to be called almost a civilization. Its people, called Elamites, lived for the most part on the Plain of Elam, an area known to the Iranians as Khuzistan. Its capital, Susa, was a large city, but for thousands of years, it was known only as a tell, a mound of rubble covered by the sands of the centuries.

Very little of the Plain of Elam has been excavated, since few have thought it worthwhile to do so, and many have feared the heat. So comparatively little is known about the people. But Elam cannot return

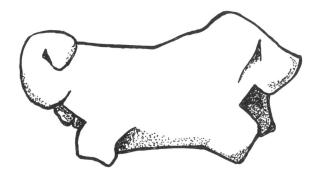

Above and below: The Dog of Jarmo. After Braidwood. (Drawings reproduced actual size of originals.)

Elamite hunts wild boar, goes naked to prove courage.

30

to its millenia of anonymity for two reasons. First, in its pictograph form of writing, the heads of domestic horses appear. Not once, but dozens of times. And so far as we know these are the earliest representations of domestic horses to be found. The horses apparently came from the highlands and were much desired by other people. Thus, they are mentioned in Elamite business deals, apparently the only written records the people made.

The second reason why Elam's anonymity had ended is evidence of the domestic dog. Among the artifacts so far discovered is a small silver amulet of a dog with a ringed tail. The amulet, dated at 2900 B.C., was probably designed to be worn upon a chain around the neck of a great lady or man.

Also, engravings showing dogs hunting deer, gazelles, and wild boar have been found. From such engravings, which have been redrawn, it appears that hunters went naked and used bow and arrow, pike and spear. About past art of animals, one has to wonder how true to life a drawing is. What points did the artist wish to stress, for instance? In these engravings the wild boar is lifelike, and in one engraving it appears that an arrow has been driven deep into the cheek and neck. A dog of giant size seems to be trying to scare the boar by attempting to look taller than it actually is. The dog is wearing a heavy collar. Were it not for the erect ears, one would suppose that it is a Mastiff, or at least an early type of Mastiff. Two other dogs also have erect ears as well as deep stops, or prominent supraorbital ridges. They have strong jaws and remarkably developed cheek muscles.

One concludes that the unknown Elamite artist portrayed two distinctive types of dogs, and provided a graphic representation of the wild boar hunts that must have been repeated many times during the Elamites' lives. One also concludes that at that time, the great families of dogs were already well on the road to completion.

Long-tailed dog amulet. Silver. Probably Elamite, end of fourth millenium B.C. The Cleveland Museum of Art. Collection of Dr. Leo Mildenberg.

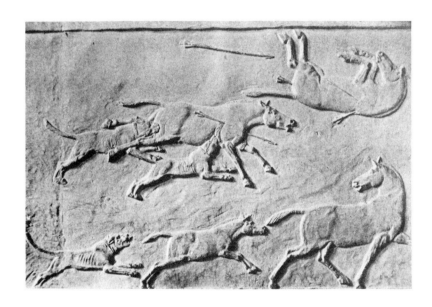

Hunting wild asses in Assyria. Note the look of terror and agony shown by the ass with the spear driven through its body and with two dogs attacking. Photo courtesy of The Metropolitan Museum of Art.

32

5.   *Dogs of Mesopotamia*

It is commonly said that civilization truly began in Mesopotamia—
with the Sumerians around 3000 B.C. Here lived the conquerors of what
then was thought to be the universe—Sargon of Akkad, Nebuchad-
nezzer, Sennacherib, Ashurnasirpal, Ashurbanipal, Hammurabi,
Tiglath-Pileser, Darius, Cyrus the Great, Xerxes, Artaxerxes, and
others.

Except for Damascus, the oldest continuously occupied city in the
world, their great cities have fallen into ruin—Ur, Uruk, Nineveh,
Babylon, Nippur. Jerusalem, younger than the others but never a capital
city of the conquerors, still survives.

The great period of Sumerian history may be roughly dated as being
between 3000 and 2000 B.C. Babylonia existed from 1900 B.C. to 600
B.C., and Assyria prevailed during roughly the same period. To simplify
Persian history, its first rise to prominence can be dated with Shilak
Inshushinak, an Elamite king who reigned in 1165 B.C. The era can be
ended with the battle of Marathon, 490 B.C., when the Athenians
stopped the advance of Darius's generals.

The Sumerians were a race of great traders. Their reed ships visited
the cities on the Indus River in Asia, stopped at the island now called
Bahrain, then went elsewhere. They were traders inland as well, visiting
the Nile over land and by ship.

They were also an agricultural nation. Their textbooks on agriculture
still survive in clay tablets, some sunbaked, some firebaked. They raised
many varieties of sheep, goats, and pigs. Unlike other nations in the area,
they enjoyed pig meat and used pork fat in cooking.

The Sumerians had guard dogs to protect their flocks and probably
herding dogs as well. For additional meat, they hunted gazelle, wild boar,
deer, and onager. The Babylonians, however, seem not to have hunted
animals to augment the meat supply from the herds.

The dogs that guarded flocks were probably of medium size and usually white. Dogs used for hunting were rather heavy-bodied, some with erect ears, other with dropped ears. The true coursing dogs were unknown to these ancient people, as were horses.

Sumerian scribes seem to have paid little attention to the shepherd dogs. This was probably caused less by their contempt for shepherds, which was the case in Egypt, and more by their living and working in cities. Then as now in Asian cities, troops of stray dogs, unowned, vermin-ridden, and always getting into trouble, annoyed the residents. Thus, the urban dwellers viewed most dogs as just troublesome pests.

Samuel Noah Kramer, greatest of the Sumerologists, cites a number of proverbs that dealt with dogs, such as "It is a dog that does not know its home," and "The smith's dog could not overturn the anvil. He (therefore) overturned the water pot instead." H. W. F. Saggs, author of *The Greatness That Was Babylon*, mentions that if an exorcist saw either a black dog or a black pig, the man would die. The Babylonians lived in fear of black dogs and of dogs urinating on them. If a white dog urinated on a man, he would fall upon hard times. But if a red dog wet upon him, the man would have happiness. Another superstition held that if a male dog mounted on a male dog, women would commit a homosexual act.

The Sumerians had a rather modern idea about crime and punishment. The law, an eye for an eye, a tooth for a tooth, became a general practice when the Semite Hammurabi became king of Babylon in 1792 B.C. He has been famed ever since as the "law giver." But under the eye for an eye law, what happens when a dog kills a man? Hammurabi's code has at least one interesting solution.

If a certified mad dog killed a free man, the dog's owner had to pay a fine of forty shekels. If the dead person was a slave, then the fine was only fifteen. It is unknown who certified the dog's madness or how madness was determined. But apparently the affliction was not caused by rabies, for that disease probably would have killed the dog before the ancient bureaucrats could have made the certification.

Babylonia, Assyria, and Persia represent raw power glorified to the utmost. Comparatively equal power has not been known either before or since. Even the dogs on the bas-reliefs represent that power. They are huge, Mastiff-like dogs with names such as "Biter of the enemy."

Because Babylonian and Assyrian artists had to portray their rulers as gods, their representations of kings are not true to life but are designed instead to strike terror in all viewers.

Yet the same artists were able to portray animals with incomparable skill. Hunted animals flee in obvious terror. A paralyzed lioness drags herself forward piteously. A lion, mortally wounded, causes shudders with its look of agony.

Dogs, too, are portrayed with unparalleled skill. They reflect the rulers who have set them on the chase. Savage brutes, they are as hungry for the kill as are their unfeeling masters. Studying the bas-reliefs makes it clear why these artists did not portray family or agricultural scenes. Their masters wanted to see only their own glory and power.

Ancient Persia, under Xerxes, Artaxerxes, and others, sent huge armies into Greece, Egypt, and Babylonia. With the armies went dogs— thousands of them—called Indian Hounds. The food sources of Babylonia were extremely rich, and under Persian rule, had to produce one-third of the food used by the empire. The Greek historian Herodotus gave the following and other figures for the period when Tritantaechmes ruled the area for the Persians. According to Herodotus, Tritantaechmes had in his private stud "besides his war horses, 800 stallions, 16,000 mares, twenty to each stallion. Besides which he kept so great a number of Indian Hounds, that four large villages of the plain were exempted from all other charges on condition of finding them food."

Xerxes would have huge caches of food stored in advance at various places along his invasion routes. Again Herodotus paints a fascinating picture, this one of the size and complexity of the army that Xerxes raised for his campaign against Greece.

Such then being the number of fighting men (2,641,616) it is my belief that the attendants who followed the camp, together with the crews of the corn barks, and of the other craft accompanying the army, made up an amount rather above than below that of the fighting men. However, I will not reckon them as either fewer or more but take them at equal number. We have therefore to add to the sum already reached an exactly equal amount. This will give 5,283,220 as the whole number of men brought by Xerxes, the son of Darius, as far as Sepias and Thermopylae.

Such then was the amount of the entire host of Xerxes. As for the number of women who ground corn, of the concubines, and the eunuchs, no one can give any sure account of it; nor can the baggage horses and other pack animals, nor the Indian Hounds which followed the army, be calculated, by reason of their multitude.

Apparently the Indian hounds were used as shield bearers, but they, or other dogs, were also used for hunting. And since hunting parties could supply fresh meat for the officers and generals, it can be said these dogs served three purposes—as shield bearers, hunters, and food suppliers. As shield bearers they had to be very large, and they had to have great courage in battle. Indeed, one can guess that they were very savage. When obtaining food, soldiers would go forth with the Hounds in a great line, flushing out any game, including lions, ahead of them. The dogs would then be loosed.

As will be explained later, the Greeks believed the Indian Hounds were crosses between bitches and tigers. They ultimately would use the Hounds in producing some of their own breeds.

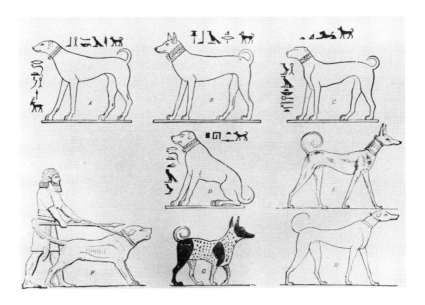

After Sir John Gardner Wilkinson. Dog F is an Assyrian of Mastiff type. Note that some dogs are pacing.

6.   The Egyptians

Our knowledge of the various types of dogs owned by the Egyptians comes mainly from tomb drawings and sculptures in Thebes, Beni Hassan, and elsewhere. Most of these were first copied in 1836 by British archaeologist Sir John Gardner Wilkinson and were first published in 1837. They have been widely copied since then, often without giving credit to Wilkinson. E. C. Ash in *Dogs, Their History and Development,* copied them without crediting Wilkinson, so that when the Fiennes copied them, they mistakenly gave credit to Ash.

One of the puzzles of civilization is that the ziggurat of Sumer, the three great pyramids of Egypt, and the great city of Mohenjo Daro in the Indus Valley of what is now Pakistan were built very early in the history of the people. Some writers have suggested, therefore, that the later history of these people actually represents periods of decadence.

Migrating people appear to have laid out a remarkable city with an enclosed underground sewer system before they entered Mohenjo Daro. The Sumerians probably came to Mesopotamia from Asia by way of the island we now know as Bahrain. Almost immediately, they built the famous ziggurat. The royal tombs with their fabulous wealth and the dozens of dead retainers date to about the same time. Pyramid building in Egypt occurred before 3000 B.C., between the Fourth and Twelfth Dynasties or from 4235 to 3064 B.C.

The Sumerians are usually credited with building the first civilization, though perhaps the early people of Mohenjo Daro and Harappa could lay equal claim to this. At any rate, the Sumerians had a written language. They left hundreds of clay tablets and from the translations we know the Sumerians had contacts with Mohenjo Daro, Bahrain, and Egypt. So we can be sure many races of dogs were well known to all three.

Painting by Peter Paul Rubens (1577-1640) of his young wife, Helen Fourment, and her dog. She became the subject of some of his masterpieces.

Above and below: Bas-relief of Hunters and Mastiffs. From the walls of Assurbanipal's palace at Nineveh 668-626 B.C. British Museum. These sculptures illustrate the raw power so typical of the rulers of the period.

Mastiffs in pursuit of lions, followed by the huntsmen.

Ancient pet dog set to guard his master's home, perhaps 3500 B.P.

40

Attic vase. Courtesy, Museum of Fine Arts, Boston. Purchased of E. P. Warren from the James Fund and Special Contribution.

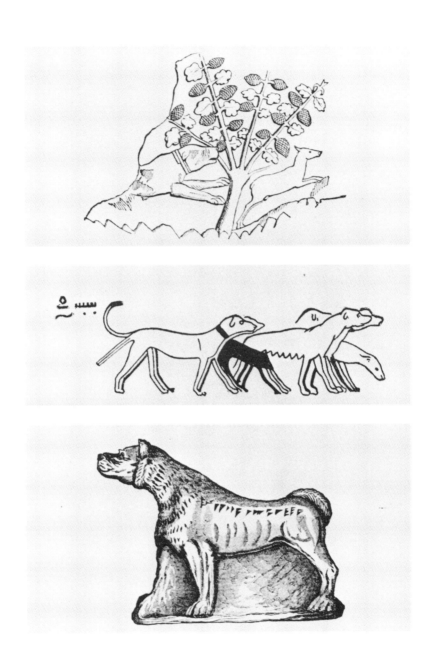

Terra cotta dog (Assyria) named "Daan Rizsu" let into a slab with hunting scene.

Servant leashes dogs and returns to royal huntsman with gazelle.

Wall painting: Apuy's house and garden. Tomb of Apuy, the Sculptor. Dynasty XIX, about 1250 B.C. The Metropolitan Museum of Art.

43

The Egyptians seem never to have gloried in sheer power as did the lion-hunting Assyrians. Although there are records of lion hunts by Egyptian pharaohs, the suspicion is that the lions released for the hunt were more or less tamed. The people undoubtedly had Mastiff-type dogs, but these do not appear to have played an important part in Egyptian life.

There were, of course, plenty of wild lions, since game populations were plentiful. But the Egyptians were interested in another kind of hunting—a different sport that has lasted to our day. This was the coursing of Greyhound-type dogs. The quarry included the gazelle, oryx, ibex, antelope, stag, the Egyptian hare, and even the ostrich. Dogs were released in pairs, as is still done to this day. When, for instance, an ibex was killed, the huntsman or his assistant would come forward, tie the legs together, and sling the ibex over the shoulder. The dogs were leashed, then they and the huntsman would return to the royal hunter.

George Rawlinson, whose book entitled *History of Ancient Egypt* was first published in 1882, wrote that in the Fourth Dynasty, only one breed of dog was known. Called the foxdog or wolf dog, it had pricked-up ears, a light body, and a stiffly curled tail. It was admitted to the house, and drawings usually show it sitting under the chair of its master. Rawlinson believed the animal was used in hunting gazelles.

The idea of only one breed appears unlikely to me, however, because it is based primarily upon the drawings and sculptures of the period. And these may have had more significance than to show one breed of dog's place in the home. Moreover, a broken sculptured tablet shows Pharaoh Antifaa, who lived during the Eleventh Dynasty, standing with four dogs. Each has its name above it plus praise for its individual qualities, and each is of a different breed.

Common names for dogs were Abu, Ken, Tarm, Akna, and Tekal. One name, Abu, translated into Blackie. The name Tekal has caused Dachshund fanciers to suppose their breed goes back to Egyptian times, since the Germans often call the Dachshund a Tekal or Tekel.

Drawings show the great coursing hounds with little or no stop, with drop ears, eyes set wide, belly well tucked up, legs long, and tails long. From such dogs have come the Saluki, Sleughi, and Rampur, other varieties of Indian coursing dogs, the Chinese Greyhound, the Afghan, and others. It is also possible that this type was spread world-wide. In which case, no dog, even of early Egyptian times, can properly be called the ancestor of all of them.

Some dogs of early Egypt had very slender muzzles, erect ears, and tightly curled tails. It is possible that these were the ancestors of the Basenji, and that population pressures pushed them deep into central Africa. Whether they barked is not known.

One breed, first shown in sculptures of the Twelfth Dynasty, has been termed the turnspit dog. Not because it is known to have operated a turnspit, but because it reminds the British of their turnspit dogs. The breed was long-bodied and short-legged. The ears were pricked, the tail long, the colors mottled.

It is probably dangerous to suppose that these sculptures and drawings are exact portraits of dogs as they were: they might be only idealizations. For example, most all of the art shows dogs with Greyhound-like tuck up or drawn-up belly. Were all dogs so made? Or does this show only an idealization based on the Egyptian love of the chase? Drawings of wolves, for instance, do not show this tuck up.

One dog is shown with a fox-like head and with a tail curled in a way that probably was never observed in any dog then or now. The curl is almost pig-like. Possibly this is an actual portrait of a dog with a broken tail. Or perhaps the artist simply was ignorant of tail curl—or careless.

Papyrus records indicate that in later periods of the Egyptian empire, wealthy people sometimes had kennels of two to three hundred hounds, and that their kennel keepers were of a very high caste. The Egyptians also raised sheep, goats, cattle, pigs, and geese. Obviously then, there were shepherd dogs. But we know little about them because herdsmen belonged to the lowest caste. And among these, swineherds were the lowest of all. Moreover, members could not escape their castes. Thus, their knowledge was passed down from father to son. The word pastor, in a sense now obsolete, covered all types or castes of herdsmen. Thus, in chapter forty-six of Genesis, Joseph says to his father and brothers, "for every shepherd is an abomination to the Egyptians." And those sculptures and drawings that have survived usually show the shepherds as being ugly and deformed.

Nonetheless, because the Egyptians were a well-settled people, it seems probable that their shepherd dogs were flock guardians rather than herding or driving dogs. They must have been large animals, since the predators of the period were lions, lynxes, and jackals. For example, in the Louvre in Paris is an Egyptian sculpture of a large, rather heavy-bodied dog. Its ears are erect and large, with one smaller than the other. The skull is large, and the muzzle strong. The tail is long. The dog is

Various types of Egyptian dogs as illustrated in ancient tombs. Copied by Sir John Gardner Wilkinson in ancient tombs in 1836.

wearing a collar from which is suspended either a bell or a tassel. This, plus the shorter ear, guarantees that the dog is sculptured from life.

It must have been a beloved family pet. Yet one is tempted to speculate that a dog of this type was a flock guardian. If the collar has a bell, then this may indicate the animal's calling. The tinkling would tell the herder the position of the dog on dark nights, and it also would tend to calm the flock.

It is well known that the Egyptians worshipped and embalmed cats, but they also embalmed dogs—many with almost the same care as was used with people. The legs were bound to the body; linen wrappings were used. The animal's face was painted on, so that both the breed and the individual could be identified.

Wilkinson opened some of these mummified dog cases. He reported that the mummies were those of the so-called fox-dog. He believed they were the ancestors of the wild red dogs that he found were so numerous in Egypt 150 years ago.

I, too, once had permission to unwrap some of these mummified dogs. I wished to measure them, to study their heads and body types, their coloration, length of hair, and so on. But when I arrived at Al-Baliana, the town railhead nearest to Abydos where I was to work, permission was suddenly withdrawn. It has never been reinstated.

Molossian Dog. Plaster reproduction of original found near Athens. Reproduction is at The Metropolitan Museum of Art in New York.

Royal Hunt. Found in the tomb of King Tut-ankh-amun in the Valley of Kings, Thebes. Egyptian XVIII Dynasty. Courtesy of The Metropolitan Museum of Art. Photograph by Harry Burton.

7.   *Dogs of the Israelites*

Terah took Abram his son and Lot the son of Haran, his grandson, and
Sarai his daughter-in-law, his son Abram's wife, and they went forth
together from Ur of the Chaldeans to go to the land of Canaan. (Gen.
11:31-32)

Abraham, or Abram as he was first known, is the progenitor of the
Hebrew race and religion. It once was estimated that he left Ur about
2000 B.C. By that date the great Sumerian nation—so often called the
first civilization—was in ruins. A new race, the Chaldeans, had moved in.
Since a Hebrew army under Abraham defeated the Hittite army of
Tid'al, a better date can be determined for Abraham. Tid'al founded a
Hittite dynasty between 1550 and 1450 B.C.

The opening passage about Abraham understates his situation. For
elsewhere in Genesis it is written that he was very rich in silver and gold
and in flocks and herds. So, too, was Lot. Both had a large retinue of
herdsmen, slaves, and soldiers. So great were their herds that they
quickly exhausted grazeable lands and had to move. Eventually, they had
to separate.

Because the Hebrews were denied entrance into Canaan, they were, to
a certain extent, nomads and wanderers. And they were strong enough to
wage war against established city states and kingdoms.

By the time they left Sumer, they must have known many kinds of
dogs, including Mastiffs and the desert Greyhounds. But as herdsmen—
or pastors, as all herder castes then were called—they must have been
interested primarily in shepherd dogs. They must have known how to
breed and develop herd guardians, such as those used to this day in the
Anatolian region of Turkey. They also would have had herd-driving dogs
as well.

Since the history of the Israelites is contained in the Old Testament,
one turns to it for information. But here one runs into a puzzle; every

mention of the dog is in some way with contempt. Earlier, in Chapter 6, I mentioned a verse from Genesis in which Joseph warns his brothers of the Egyptians' contempt for shepherds. Joseph had become the Pharaoh's regent or at least his major administrator. A second famine occurs and again the Israelites go down to Egypt. Joseph warns as follows:

> When Pharaoh calls you and says: "What is your occupation?" you shall say, "Your servants have been keepers of cattle from our youth even until now, both we and our fathers," in order that you may dwell in the land of Goshen; for every shepherd is an abomination to the Egyptians. (Gen. 46:33-34)

Since the Israelites were basically shepherds at the time, they couldn't have had contempt for themselves. Their contempt for dogs may simply have been an attitude they absorbed from the Egyptians during their two sojourns in Egypt. Later, when they were established in villages and cities in their own land and only a few of them were shepherds, this contempt grew.

Finally, homeless dogs—the pariah dogs of the desert areas—lived outside the cities and villages. These, as well as jackals, dug up the graves of the dead and fed upon the corpses. Moreover, they may have fed upon the bodies of homeless beggars, lepers, and criminals, which were carried into the desert and left stranded. So whatever their feelings for family pets or shepherd dogs, the Israelites could have only contempt for animals that fed upon human bodies. This contempt continued even into New Testament times, although by then it seems somewhat tempered. Matthew, Chapter 15, tells of how a Canaanite woman, hoping to have her daughter healed, follows the disciples and finally worships at the feet of Jesus. The disciples want Jesus to chase her away, and He, in fact, says, "I was sent only to the lost sheep of Israel. It is not right to take the children's bread and toss it to the dogs."

"Yes, Lord," she says, "but even the dogs eat the crumbs that fall from their master's table." To which Jesus replies, "Oh woman of great faith! Your request is granted."

In his reply, Jesus seems to be likening the Canaanites to dogs, as does the woman in her humble reply. Whether it also indicates that either the Israelites or the Canaanites had pet dogs is impossible to say. It is possible that scavenger dogs hung about the homes hunting for bits of food, and that they were barely tolerated.

It is strange that one has to wait nearly 1200 years to find a story in which Jesus shows pity and understanding for the sufferings of dogs. Stranger still is that the story is based on an Islamic tradition. The Persian poet, Nizami, is the author of the classic love story, *Laila and Majnun* (or *Laili and Majnun*). Before he died in 1203, Nizami wrote a poem that tells the following story about Jesus, called The Eye of Charity.

Jesus lingers in the market place one evening "teaching the people parables of truth and grace." There is a commotion nearby, and Jesus "and his meek disciples" go to investigate. A crowd has gathered near the body of a dead dog lying in the gutter. Some throw rocks at it, some hold their noses, some turn away. Others begin to shout. "'Detested creature! He pollutes the earth and air!' 'His eyes are blear!' 'His ears are foul!' 'His ribs are bare!' 'In his torn hide there's not a decent shoe string left!' 'No doubt the execrable cur was hung for theft!'"

But Jesus spoke "and dropped this saving wreath upon it": "Even pearls are dark before the whiteness of his teeth." The crowd, ashamed, melts away, and one observer says, "No creature so accursed can be but some good thing a loving eye can see."

Among the questions that remain, two seem important. Did the Israelites have and use hunting dogs? And did they have house pets? They had come from Chaldea where hunting dogs were used. The Babylonians, Assyrians, and Egyptians also used hunting dogs, and the Israelites had close albeit unpleasant associations with them.

The Old Testament is silent on both questions. But in Genesis 27:2, Isaac commands Esau, "Now then, take your weapons, your quiver, and your bow, and go out to the field and hunt game for me, and prepare for me some savory food such as I love."

What! No dog? Could Esau have killed a gazelle without using a dog? The answer is yes, certainly. Ice Age hunters had supplied themselves with meat before the domestication of any animal and even before the invention of the bow and arrow. Also, Esau would not have been hunting alone. He would have taken along a dozen of his servants and slaves. The hunt would not have been easy without dogs, but that may have added to the rites of celebration.

Another passage, Proverbs 30:29-31, is also worth mentioning. Some translations of it have used the word Greyhound. Yet the Greyhound was unknown in Mesopotamia at that time, unless the word refers to the Egyptian coursing dogs. This theory is untenable, however, as Greek and

Roman texts will later show. The New International translation of the Bible is, I think, closer to the truth. It uses lion instead of Greyhound, and the entire passage reads as follows:

There are three things that are stately in their stride, four that move with stately bearing: a lion, mighty among beasts, who retreats before nothing; a strutting rooster; a he-goat; and a king with his army around him.

What, then, is the answer to this puzzle? First, the Israelites were shepherds. They had immense flocks of sheep, goats, and cattle, so they had a ready supply of meat. Killing wild beasts for food was not necessary. But as the story of Isaac and Esau seems to indicate, gazelle or oryx meat might have been reserved for festival occasions.

Second, the people's contempt for dogs, even from the times of Jericho and Joshua, must certainly have been strengthened by their stay in Egypt. And finally, their long years of wandering and their captivity must have given them an abhorrence of sports, including hunting. The problems of their lives must always have caused them to couple sports with their hated enemies.

In the King James Bible, Deuteronomy 23:18 reads, "Thou shalt not bring the hire of a whore, or the price of a dog, into the house of the Lord thy God for any vow: for both these are abominations unto the Lord thy God." Some writers take this to mean that the Israelites bought and sold dogs, and that they probably had home pets as well. The Revised Standard Version makes this somewhat clearer, saying, "There shall be no cult prostitute of the daughters of Israel, neither shall there be a cult prostitute of the sons of Israel. You shall not bring the hire of a harlot, or the wages of a dog, into the house of the Lord your God in payment for any vow; for both of these are an abomination to the Lord your God."

To best understand this passage, it is necessary to refer to Babylonian religious rites. A priestess of Babylon might reserve herself solely to service for a god. Or she might serve men by copulating with anyone who asked her to do so. Hence, she was a cult prostitute in the eyes of the Israelites. Also, it seems that male temple workers were eunuchs and, as such, would be abominable to the Israelites. Indeed, Deuteronomy 23:1 reads, "He whose testicles are crushed, or whose male member is cut off shall not enter the assembly of the Lord." The epithet to describe such a man would be "dog." (It should be remembered that in ancient civilizations, including Rome, a man swore on his testicles, which could be cut off if he lied. The word testify has its origin in that custom.)

Thus, I do not think the passages have anything to do with dogs. And this seems to be supported by the translation given in the New International Version, which reads, "No Israelite man or woman is to become a temple prostitute. You must not bring the earnings of a female prostitute or a male prostitute into the house of the Lord your God to pay any vow, because the Lord your God detests them both."

To conclude, I do not believe there is any evidence that the Israelites ever used dogs for hunting. Nor do I believe they ever had pet dogs, as such. Since many of their shepherd dogs were guardians of flocks, the animals might also have been used as house guardians. They would have been excellent at keeping wandering pariah dogs from the house. But I must caution that this is only a supposition, and it cannot be backed up by actual evidence.

Attic Shepherd Dog. Note corded coat as in modern Komondorok and Pulik. British Museum copyright.

53

Actaeon being destroyed by his hounds. He had chanced to see the virgin goddess Artemis as she bathed. Enraged, she turned him into a stag, so that his own dogs killed him.

8.   *Dogs of the Greeks*

And lo, a hound raised up his head and pricked his ears, even where he lay, Argos, the hound of Odysseus, of the hardy heart, which of old himself had bred but had got no joy of him, for ere that, he went to sacred Ilios . . . .

There lay Argos, full of vermin. Yet even now when he was ware of Odysseus standing by, he wagged his tail and dropped both ears, but nearer to his master he had not now the strength to draw. But Odysseus looked aside and wiped away a tear that he easily hid from Eumaeus, and straightaway asked him . . . .

"Then didst thou make answer swineherd Eumaeus:
'In very truth is the dog of a man that has died in a far land. If he were what he once was in limb and in the feats of the chase, when Odysseus left him to go to Troy, soon wouldst thou marvel at the sight of his swiftness and his strength. There was no beast that could flee from him in the deep places of the wood, when he was in pursuit; for even on a track he was the keenest hound.

'But now he is holden in an evil case, and his lord hath perished far from his own country . . . .' But upon Argos came the fate of the black death even in the hour that he beheld Odysseus again, in the twentieth year." (Homer, *The Odyssey*)

It is not certain when Homer lived, though it now is thought to have been sometime between 800 and 700 B.C. Even his place of birth is unknown. What is certain is that Homer knew something about dogs and hunting, and his tales recount the deeds of heroes who lived 300 years or more earlier. Except for one reference, to be discussed later, Homer's *Iliad* and *Odyssey* are the first books in Greek history to mention dogs.

Greek warrior with dog. Note similarity of the crouching dog to Acropolis Museum Dog (page 59). British Museum copyright.

Greek huntsman. Attic vase. Courtesy
Museum of Fine Arts, Boston. Francine
Bartlett Donation. Purchased of E. P.
Warren.

Bilingual cup with dog, in Tondo. Earthenware. Fired orange. Attic, ca. 525-520 B.C. The Cleveland Museum of Art. Collection of Dr. Leo Mildenberg.

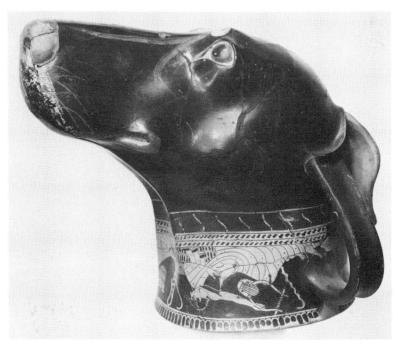

Head of Laconian Hound, ca. 500-490 B.C. Courtesy of Soprintendenza Alle Antichita, Dell Etruria Meridionale.

58

BEGGING DOG. Bronze with minute traces of gold leaf. Late Hellenistic or early Roman, second to first century, B.C. The Cleveland Museum of Art. Collection of Dr. Leo Mildenberg.

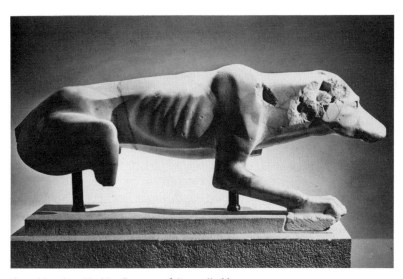

Crouching dog. Marble. Courtesy of Acropolis Museum.

The earliest civilization in ancient Greece was that of the Minoans on Crete from approximately 3000 to 1500 B.C. Cretan civilization collapsed suddenly following a disaster of such magnitude that its full nature is still not known.

The first Greek-speaking people, the Mycenae, entered the area from the north. They succeeded the Minoans of Crete and assimilated much of their culture. Their great power came between 1600 and 1100 B.C., a period that has sometimes been called the "Dark Ages of Greece" because so little is known about it.

Archaeologists have made startling discoveries in this land, including tablets obtained from ruined palaces. The Mycenae wrote in what has been called Linear B script, and this was deciphered in 1952 by Michael Ventris, with assistance from John Chadwick. The tablets were only the journals of clerks. But they told something of the people's daily lives since they contained records of food, livestock, wool, leather goods, and so on. Chadwick did find one reference which could indicate that the Mycenae had dogs and that they used them to hunt deer, if not other animals. The word was "hunters," which in Greek, reports Chadwick, literally means "dog leaders."

From Mycenae, Agamemnon led his Greeks to the siege of Troy. The *Iliad* concerns the last year of the ten-year siege; the *Odyssey* tells of Odysseus's struggles to return to his home. He finally gets back after twenty years of wandering. Many evil and powerful men are attempting to marry his wife, Penelope, and to steal his estates. He comes disguised as a beggar and not even his wife recognizes him. But Argos does. Argos, now more than twenty years old, neglected, covered with vermin, lying on a dunghill! Odysseus dares not greet the old dog, and Argos dies.

The "Dark Age of Greece" ended when a new wave of Greek-speaking people came from the north. They were the Dorians, and their surge toward power can roughly be dated as beginning in 700 B.C. European Greece is mountainous, and its soil is poor. The Dorian Greeks multiplied so rapidly that the land could not support all of them. They became a maritime power, setting up colonies from the Black Sea to Spain and on all of the islands in the Aegean Sea. However, there was no real central power. The colonies were city states whose people called themselves Hellenes. But each colony was extremely jealous of the other. In their continuing arguments, some formed alliances, and these were continually changing.

Most of what we know about Greek dogs comes from Xenophon, who wrote a remarkable treatise on hunting called the *Cynegeticus*. It is a study of the hunting dogs of his time, the breeds, their breeding, feeding, and training. In a roundabout way, something is learned about shepherd dogs from Theocritus. He was the first and possibly the greatest of all idyllic poets, and he wrote at approximately the beginning of the second century B.C. Xenophon was born about 430 B.C. of aristocratic parents at Scillus in Ellis, not far from Olympia. He died about 370 B.C., probably at Corinth. Xenophon might have become a philosopher. He studied with Socrates, who urged this course for him, but he preferred being a soldier. His writings tell of him fighting with his own Athenians and with the Persian, Xerxes; being deserted by the Persians in a strange land; leading the remainder of the Greek army on a long march to the sea; trying to found a colony; fighting for Sparta; and being exiled from Athens and then pardoned.

When he was exiled, the Spartans gave Xenophon a home. There he settled down to the life of a country gentleman and wrote many of his historical works. He spent much of his time hunting, and it was probably in Sparta that Xenophon wrote his *Cynegeticus*.

Raw power had been the outstanding feature of Assryian and Babylonian sculpture. Mighty kings were shown, hunting nothing less than lions, or, what might have been just as exciting, chasing and killing onagers. But the Greeks had a sense of democracy, even if they had an aristocracy. Moreover, no lions were left in the territory of the Hellenes. There were deer and gazelles, but the country was mountainous, and coursing never seems to have been popular.

Still Xenophon believed that the hunting sports were absolutely necessary as a preliminary to soldiering. While this attitude was common among the Athenians, it was almost a religion for the Spartans. And Xenophon lived and wrote among the Spartans. The hunting sports taught skill with weapons, agility in going over rough ground, and obedience to teachers; they developed strength and endurance. The quarry? Chiefly the hare, but also deer and wild boar. The latter were extremely dangerous animals, and only the brave and strong dared to challenge them on foot.

Other writers followed Xenophon, copying his *Cynegeticus* and adding to it. Some were Greeks, others Romans. They include Arrian, Julius Pollux, Oppian, Gratius, and Nemesianus.

Arrian (Flavius Arrianus), the first Greek to be given a Roman military command, was born in Bithynia in A.D. 96 and died about 180. He was one of the great men of his time. He studied under the famous Epictetus, and only his notes remain of the master's works. As a military commander, Arrian won a great victory over the Alans, and he served as Archon of Athens. He published his own *Cynegeticus*.

Julius Pollux, or Polydeuces, wrote from the Greek trading city of Naucratis on the Canopic branch of the Nile in Egypt, and later in Athens. He wrote history's first dictionary, a ten-volume work called the *Onomasticon*. He lived in the second century A.D.

It is now believed that there were two Oppians—that it was the first who wrote a 3500-line poem on fishing and died of the plague at age thirty, and that it was a second Oppian who wrote a Cynegetica of 2150 lines sometime after 211. Both poems are in hexameter, with the Cynegetica being inferior to the other.

Gratius was a Roman poet who lived at the time of Augustus. Only a fragment of 541 hexameter lines remains of his Cynegeticus. He described various kinds of hunting, game, and the best kinds of dogs and horses.

Nemesianus, a Roman poet born at Carthage in 283, was popular at the court of Emperor Carus. Only 325 hexameter lines remain of his Cynegeticus.

Of the more than a dozen breeds mentioned by these writers, only a few need be mentioned here. Several will be listed in the section under Roman dogs. However, it is important to point out that various breeds were being developed in all the lands known to the Greeks. Many of them were fully developed and not merely in some stage of it. Moreover, it will be shown later that dogs were, by Greek times, known to all the world.

The Greek dogs can be divided into three groups: hunting dogs, guard and shepherd dogs, and household pets. The most important dogs in the first group were the Indian Hound, and the Laconian or Spartan; in the second, the Molossian; and in the third, the Melitaean or Maltese.

Hunting Dogs

The Indian Hounds that accompanied Xerxes and his army were mentioned in Chapter 5. One belief was that this breed resulted from crossing a bitch dog with a male tiger. When in season, the bitch was tied out in the forest where the tiger could find her. He might devour her or mate her. The former was probably his usual procedure. But if he mated her, the first and second generations were said to be savage. The third generation, however, could be trained for hunting.

Another writer, named Nicander, is quoted by Pollux as saying that the Indian Hounds descended from the dogs of Actaeon. The tragic story of Actaeon was a favorite of the Greeks and Romans, and they pictured the incident of his death on vases and mosaics and in sculpture. The latter provides a reasonable idea of the size of the dogs.

According to legend, Actaeon took his hounds—Raven, Snatcher, Bright Eyes, and Wolf Howl—on a stag hunt. But in some sylvan glade he surprised the goddess Artemis, who was nude in her bath. Angry, she changed him into a stag, whereupon his dogs attacked and killed him. Nicander claimed that the four dogs then recovered from their "madness," crossed the Euphrates, and wandered into India. There they became the foundation stock for the Indian Hound.

According to Pollux, Alexander the Great had an Indian Hound named Peritar that was said to have conquered a lion. In admiration for the dog's courage and ability, Alexander founded a city and named it for the dog. If this is so, the city has vanished with the centuries. After the death of Alexander, Ptolomy, his general, set up a monarchy in Egypt. Philostratus wrote that at his triumphal parade, Ptolomy II had 2400 dogs in the march, most of which were Indian Hounds.

Laconia was the ancient name for the southwestern district of the Peloponnesus. Homer writes that Laconia was the realm of the Achaean prince, Menelaus. It was conquered by the Dorians about 1100 B.C., and thereafter, its capital was Sparta. The most famous hunting dog of antiquity was the Laconian or Spartan. According to Xenophon, there were two varieties, a large dog and a smaller one. The large one was sometimes called the Castorian, being named after one of the twins, Castor and Pollux. In Greek mythology, they were sons of Zeus, who, in the guise of a swan, impregnated Leda.

The smaller Laconian, or Spartan, was called the Vulpine, since it was said to have resulted from crossing a dog and a fox. The two strains apparently merged into one. The exact size of the Laconians cannot be determined, but Denison Bigham Hull, author of *Hounds and Hunting in Ancient Greece,* guessed that they were about eighteen inches tall at the shoulder and that they probably weighed thirty to forty pounds.

Around 1900, a statue of Actaeon was on exhibit at New York's Metropolitan Museum of Art. The statue showed a Laconian stretching up the naked leg of Actaeon, as stag horns begin to sprout from the latter's skull. Based upon this, and some measurements of one of our farm dogs, Hull must be close to correct.

About the Laconians, Aristotle commented that both sexes were fit for breeding at six months. The gestation period was sixty days—sometimes 59 or even 63—and the bitch usually averaged eight pups per litter. The normal life span for males was ten years and bitches twelve; but some, he said, managed to reach twenty. Hard work, said Aristotle, made a male a more vigorous stud.

As Xenophon describes it, the Laconian was soundly built, as becomes a hunting dog, but was light in muzzle and had small prick ears. The belly showed considerable tuck up; the tail was long and tended to show a slight curl. The coat was fine and dense, with no hair at all on the back of the ears. The colors were black and tan, and tan and white. There may have been slight markings of white, but if so, Xenophon doesn't say.

Shepherd Dogs

And the dogs and the herdsmen stayed behind to guard the steading.
(Homer, *The Odyssey*)

Suppose we call that goatherd hither. See? A young white dog at his kids barks lustily.

Spare wolf, my sheep, nor injure me
Because I may tend though small I be.

Sleepest, Lamprinus? Up! No dog should sleep
That with the shepherd-boy attends his sheep.
(Theocritus, *Daphnis and Menalcas*)

Literature of the Greeks is as scanty on the subject of shepherd dogs as is that of the Egyptians and Israelites. The above passages, give clues.

Shepherds and shepherd dogs were generally despised. In Sparta, the farmers were called helots, or slaves, and it was said that they wore dogskin caps. This was sufficient to bring contempt from the aristocrats, even if it was not strictly true.

It is obvious from the quotation from Homer that the shepherd dogs were flock guardians. As such, they would guard against strangers, as well as against wandering stray dogs, wolves, and men bent upon stealing parts of the flocks. They could at least alert the herdsmen.

That young shepherd dogs would live with the sheep, grow up playing with the lambs, perhaps thinking of themselves as sheep, or at least a part of the flock, seems indicated from the first quotation from Theocritus.

64

And the dog is white. This conforms well with what is known today of the guardian flock dogs of the Balkans and Anatolia. White dogs blended with the color of the animals at night. Black dogs did not and could scare the animals. (The banning of white dogs by national German Shepherd clubs therefore seems a little ridiculous.)

The shepherd boys and girls played flute music to calm the sheep. Indeed, the theme of Daphnis and Menalcus is a flute-playing contest. In Longus' idyllic novel, *Daphnis and Chloe,* Daphnis is able to call his animals with flute music. He also boasts that he has not lost a single animal to a wolf, nor have his animals destroyed a single garden.

It is not clear whether the Greeks had driving and herding dogs in addition to their guard dogs. But it is certain they had dogs that could fiercely fight intruders, be they human or animal. Yet they were gentle with the herds and herdsmen, and as nearly as we can be certain of anything, the dogs were either purebred Molossians or at least of Molossian background. Little is known of the Molossian's ancestry. Legend has it that it descends from a dog named Laelaps. Hephaestus forged Laelaps from Demonesian bronze, put a soul into it, and gave it to Zeus. After numerous owners, it was turned to stone, but presumably not before it had sired a race of mighty dogs.

Earlier, I pointed out that some dogs migrated from their point of origin, probably in central Asia, into the high mountains of Tibet. There they moved toward giantism, as did so many mammals of the late Pleistocene epoch. The dog the Greeks called the Molossian may have evolved during this time.

I believe there were originally two types of Molossians. One had a far wider jaw or muzzle than the other. It was shorter, often undershot. The second had the longer, narrower muzzle that is associated with the Molossians shown in Greek sculpture. The broader muzzled dogs were taken to Mesopotamia; the others to Greece. The former became the ancestor of all the Mastiff-type dogs plus the longer, boxlike muzzled sporting dogs. The path of travel was over the ancient "silk route." But at some point, several of the Mastiff-type dogs were diverted along a more northerly course to the Celtic lands. And from there they were taken to Britain.

Put in simpler terms, based on skull and muzzle structure, as well as size, all the world's Mastiff-type dogs and most or all of the sporting dogs descend from Tibetan stock by way of the Molossian. More is written about this evolution in the chapter on Tibet.

Pet Dogs

The pet dog most often mentioned by ancient writers is the Melitaen, and this they assume to have been a Maltese. A painting of one appears on a Grecian vase displayed in the British Museum.

The Greeks, more than any other people until the present, portrayed dogs in their art. They appear in vase paintings, sculptures, and mosaics, and they are pictured in marvelous detail. The artists, particularly the sculptors, portrayed them naturally. One sees a dog scratching for fleas, another obviously sick, and to this day they evoke sympathy.

The dogs are almost always either Laconian or Molossian, although an occasional example of a Greyhound-type dog appears. And I once saw a Grecian vase with a picture of a Pomeranian-type dog.

The Pomeranian belongs to the northern-type dogs. Possibly it was brought from China over the silk route. In any event, it seems certain that dwarf dogs were known from early times in many parts of the world.

One of the first Greeks to attempt a sort of fiction was a writer named Alciphron. Almost nothing is known about him, neither where nor when he was born. But some of his *Letters From the Country and the Town, of Fishermen, Farmers, Parasites, and Courtesans* have survived. In number 19 of these, a tenant farmer resolves to use a spring trap to catch a fox that is stealing grapes from the vines.

I set a trap the other day for those filthy foxes with a piece of meat on the spring . . . . So I made up my mind to catch the thieving fox and hand her over to my master. But she never came near the trap. It was our little Maltese dog Plangon whom we were rearing as a toy to please the mistress, who got caught. The greedy little creature came after the meat: and now for three days has been lying dead and is beginning to stink.*

Alciphron was obviously writing from experience, so it must be assumed that the Greeks also kept dogs as pets. Yet an interesting question complicates this fact: Were the dogs of the Greeks savage? Were they still only half domesticated as some writers have suggested? Certainly, the opening lines of Homer's *Iliad* suggest that they were:

*Note: Alciphron probably lived in the second century A.D. He wrote in purest Attic style, and while his letters are fictitious, in the sense that the authors are imaginary, they give a very broad picture of Greek life, as their titles suggest. His letters from courtesans are particularly valuable to scholars.

66

Sing, O goddess, the anger of Achilles, son of Peleus, that brought countless ills upon the Achaeans. Many a brave soul did it send hurrying down to Hades, and many a hero did it yield a prey to dogs and vultures, for so were the counsels of Jove fulfilled from the day on which the son of Atreus, king of men, and great Achilles, first fell out with one another.

R. H. A. Merlen, lecturer in anatomy at the Royal Veterinary College in England and author of *De Canibus*, gives several examples that indicate the dogs of the Greeks may have been savage. One is the story of Actaeon, turned into a stag by Artemis and then killed by his hounds. But one can object that Actaeon, turned into a stag, would smell like a stag and could reasonably be expected to be killed by his dogs.

Dr. Merlen then quotes a portion of Homer in which King Priam of Troy cries out in despair for himself and, I suspect, for the people of Troy, not the least of which were his fifty sons and numerous daughters.

And when someone's sword has laid me dead, I shall be torn to pieces by the ravening dogs at my door. The very dogs I have fed at table and trained to watch my gate, will loll in front of it, maddened by their master's blood.

It seems to me that Priam may have meant more than his dogs. He may have been thinking of those among his people who would betray him. It is true that Oriental cities were then and are today cursed by droves of starving, vermin-ridden, half-savage dogs. A mob of such animals surely hung about the gates of Priam's palace. Undoubtedly he fed some of them, and they then staked out a territory around the door. They would be tolerated because they would bark at night and signal the approach of strangers. But these dogs would not be Priam's hunting dogs, nor those of his shepherds.

At one point in the *Iliad,* Priam and Achilles make a truce so that each side can bury their dead. Achilles allows King Priam to take the body of his son Hector for proper burial. Yet as Homer says in the opening lines of the *Iliad,* bodies of the dead were given to dogs and vultures.

In the end, King Priam, old and very weak, was slain by a son of Achilles, who cut off Priam's head. The body was dragged away and placed upon the grave of Achilles.

Mosaic from Carthage, showing heavy, blunt-nosed, short-eared dogs taking part in a boar hunt. Dogs' ears may have been cropped. Courtesy Musee du Bardo.

9.   *Africa*

North Africa was closely allied to Greece and Rome in many ways, particularly in their dogs and horses and the use of mosaics. The Greeks had developed the art of mosaics to a remarkable degree. Both the Romans and the North Africans either developed their own mosaicists or imported artists from Greece. The Carthaginians, the Libyans, and the Tunisians used mosaics to picture their dogs. The war dogs on the frieze of the Altar of Zeus in Anatolia have already been mentioned. All North Africa knew and used the desert coursing dogs of the Egyptians and probably the Vertragi of the Celts. Arrian, writing of the fast Libyan horses, tells of youngsters riding without using bridles, controlling the animals by guiding their heads with sticks. He says that the horses, fast as they were, could not run down a gazelle. But they could run down the wild asses, or onagers, which tired rapidly. The Egyptians, too, had coursed the onagers.

Arrian does not say so, but since the Libyans had the fast desert hounds, it seems certain that both hounds and horses were used in gazelle hunting. Some of the dogs may well have been crosses between the Egyptian dogs—possible ancestors of the modern breeds of Saluki, Sleughi, and others—and the Celtic Greyhounds.

The radiation theory that was mentioned earlier contends that the world became populated when primitive peoples on the fringes of cultural centers were forced farther and farther from the center. Whatever the method of migration, it remains true that the most primitive people went to the ends of the earth. Some of them developed high cultures of their own. But in any case, they took along their dogs.

One primitive dog was, and is, the Basenji. It shares several common features with some of the wild canids. It does not bark, and it comes into estrus only once a year instead of the normal twice. These characteristics also are shared with the Dingo of Australia.

Some of the dogs of the Egyptians appear to have Basenji characteristics. We cannot be sure of the exact relationship, if any, because there are no records of such features as those listed above. And there is no certain indication as to size. On the other hand, I have seen dogs of Basenji type that vary greatly in size in widely separated areas of equatorial Africa.

If, in fact, the domestic dog became a true dog in Asia, then it is likely that the Basenji followed the migratory route down the Indus to Mohenjo Daro, Bahrain, Sumeria, and then to the Nile. The time would have been a pre-dynastic period in Egypt.

The plains and semidesert areas are the habitat of the lion and the leopard, the jackal and the baboon. The Basenji could not have survived there. It would have to have moved on, either with migrating people or with traders, and the route probably was the Nile. Eventually, the Basenji would find a home in Central Africa.

Once, during the final years of the Belgians in the Congo, now Zaire, I asked Belgian officials to take me to tribes that had the Basenji dogs. They seemed puzzled. The conversation went something like this:

"Do you mean the dogs that do not bark?"

"Yes," I answered.

"Well, we can take you up country to see them. You will have to go by plane and river launch. But please do not use that word, basenji. In their language it means savage, and if you use the word, and they think you are talking about them, you might get a spear in your back."

"What do they call the dogs?"

"Saba Dogs. It means Dogs of the Queen of Sheba."

I did go to see the dogs. They were smaller than those I had seen in Ghana and the Gold Coast, and more like one I had seen in Liberia in 1934. Later, in Nairobi, I met Dr. Louis Leakey, who, besides being a dog judge, was a world-famous paleoanthropologist (one who studies fossils).

Dr. Leakey had collected some of the dogs which were sent to England around 1950. He, too, objected to the name Basenji, saying that it could be translated as Dog of the Forest. Another translated it as "Bush Thing." Thus, different tribes had different names for these dogs.

As with all other breeds, modern dog fanciers have refined the Basenji. And, as they have done with other breeds, people have taken the dogs wherever they themselves have wandered. It therefore is not uncommon to see them in the contrasting climates of Alaska and Scandinavia.

70

Hunting rabbits (above) and fox (below) in this mosaic from Musee du Bardo, Tunis, Tunisia. Upper dog is named Ederatus, lower dog Mystela. Mosaic is late Greek or early Roman.

71

Greyhounds At Play. Early Roman or Greek. Courtesy Vatican Museum.

10.   *The Romans*

It is difficult to separate the Greek and Roman worlds, since they were interlocked in so many ways. The Romans conquered Greece. But rich Romans sent their sons to be educated in Athens. And Greek slaves or freedmen served as tutors for Roman children. Greece had made contacts with the countries on both sides of the Mediterranean and inland to the Black Sea and Persia. Rome sent its legions into most of Europe and into the British Isles.

There, the Romans encountered the Celts. To them, the Celts were barbarians, and in actuality they were. Yet they had a profound influence upon Rome and its dogs. For this reason, the Celts will be discussed in a special section.

A comparison may be made between the sports of the Greeks and the Romans. The Greeks enjoyed what now are called track and field sports. The athletes were men and they competed in the nude. The Romans gloried in the cruel, bloody sports of the arena, including chariot racing with horses and dogs. The Romans, despite their depravity in later years, were in some ways prudes. Their censors required that the pubic area of Praxiteles' great statue, Venus of Cnidus, be covered with a metal draping.

The Greeks made hare hunting something of an art. While boar hunting was a dangerous sport, they used it to train young men for war. The Romans tended to blitz an area, even though this might end hunting in that section for years to come. Some, at least, did consider hunting a healthful sport that might keep young men from immorality. Yet during the Roman reign, more authors wrote about hunting and dogs than had the Greeks at the height of their power.

73

Pagan Roman soldier is converted, and becomes Saint Eustace when the stag he is chasing turns and displays a crucifix and figure of Christ growing from its head. His dogs will not attack the stag. Later Saint Eustace and family are thrown to wild beasts which will not touch them. Several hundred years later, the same story is told of Saint Hubert. Painting by Pisamello about 1450. Courtesy of The National Gallery, London.

Pet Dog: Painting in a wall frieze, House of the Epigrams, Pompeii. Volcano destroyed Pompeii in A.D. 79. Drawing by Dean Harris.

75

Beware The Dog (*Cave Canem*). Mosaic showing a guard dog chained to the door. From Pompeii. Courtesy Archaeological Museum, Naples.

The ancient world was fascinated by the story of Actaeon being turned into a stag, and then killed by his own dogs. This picture is from a wall scene in a home at Pompeii. Courtesy Archaeological Museum, Naples.

Ruined wall painting from Pompeii, A.D. 79. Courtesy Archaeological Museum, Naples.

RUNNING DOG WITH SILVER EYES. Bronze, eyes inlaid with silver. Roman, A.D. first to second century. The Cleveland Museum of Art. Collection of Dr. Leo Mildenberg.

BLACK GLAZED DOG. ASKOS. Possibly early Pug type. Apulian, ca. 320-290 B.C. The Cleveland Museum of Art. Collection of Dr. Leo Mildenberg.

Painting on a wall in Pompeii, the city destroyed by a volcano in A.D. 79. Courtesy of the Archaeological Museum, Naples.

Molossian Hound, Bronze. Roman, A.D. second to third century. The Cleveland Museum of Art. Collection of Dr. Leo Mildenberg.

By late Roman times, the ancestors of most of the dogs known today were present in Italy. A possible exception was the Nordic or Spitz type of large dog, although lap dogs of that type were known. The Romans knew the Molossians, the great Mastiffs of Assyria and Babylon, the Indian dogs of India and Persia, Greyhound types, the huge Irish dogs that were brought down from Britain, the Cretan hounds that may be the ancestors of Bloodhounds and Bassets and others. The British claim their land is the birthplace of the terriers. In fact, they will not use the term terrier except for British dogs or those developed from British terriers. Yet dogs of definite terrier type were in Rome.

Among the Great Roman writers who provided information on dogs are some who are still considered immortal masters of literature and thought: One was Vergil, author of the *Aeneid*, the *Eclogues*, and *Georgics*. He was born in 70 B.C. Another was Lucretius, author of *On the Nature of Things*, who was born in 98 B.C. and died in 55 B.C.

There was Horace, a friend and contemporary of Vergil; it is said that Latin lyric poetry died with him. Still another writer was Martial, famed epigrammatist who could be obscene but whose delicate poem to a dog will be quoted later. Martial was born in Spain about A.D. 38 and died in A.D. 102.

There were others, too—authors of lesser note and often copiers of Xenophon, but they still shed great light on the dogs of the times and their uses. Among them, Arrian, Oppian, Gratius, and Nemesianus are described in the earlier discussion of the Greeks. Dio Cassius (Cassius Dio Cocceanus)* tells how dogs were used for pulling carts and even for chariot racing in the arena. And Plutarch, the great historian, tells of performing dogs, including one remarkable animal in particular.

Some of the period's authors give only clues to dogs while focusing on pictures of Roman life. These include Petronius, author of the *Satyricon*; Claudian; Aelian; and others.

In the *Satyricon*, Petronius describes in great detail the banquet given by Trimalchio, a millionaire and freed slave. During the long, drawn out, drunken brawl, Trimalchio has what appears to be a dead wild boar carried in, while a Laconian hound dashes around the table, roaring and upsetting guests. A servant, simulating the hunter, then stabs the simulated boar, spilling out food.

Elsewhere in the *Satyricon*, Petronius tells of a favorite child slave of Trimalchio. He has infected eyes and stained teeth, and is sitting on the

*Translated by Troy, Loeb Classical Library.

80

floor wrapping a green shawl about a disgustingly fat lap dog. He is trying to force half a loaf of bread down the dog's throat, although the poor animal seems to want to throw up.

This gives Trimalchio an idea, and he has a porter bring in his huge mastiff on a leash. The servant kicks the dog to make it lie down by Trimalchio, who then boasts about the mastiff. This makes Croesus, the child slave, jealous. He sets the lap dog near the big dog and sics it on to yap at the mastiff. The latter nearly tears the little dog to pieces. We never learn whether it survives.

Claudian, writing on the consulship of the brilliant Roman general Stilicho, says, "The gods discover for thee plots against thy life, and lead thee to the very lair of treason even as Molossian hounds guide the huntsman with their subtle scent." Stilicho was later charged with treason, probably unfairly, and was executed in 408.

In Aelian's *Letters of Farmers,* there is one which is satyric in tone. It reads, in part, as follows:

I am going to nail up the hare's skin, Lamprias, so that it may be a monument of your prowess in the chase—like those mighty hunters of old, you know. And your success in hunting shall be recorded in writing also. Did you take it yourself, or did you receive him as a gift? And how was he caught sight of to begin with, the tiny thing: The dogs must really have had keen scent; they couldn't have seen him—they must have smelled him out.

If Aelian's letter is barbed, there is another, written in the fourth century by Symmachus to some young men, which praises much as Xenophon had done. Symmachus had received the trophy of the hunt, and he will nail it on the threshold where it can be admired for years—a habit that still exists today.

Your hunting bears witness to your fulness of strength and vigor. So this is my first reason for pleasure about you. The second stage of my happiness is that I should have deserved what you took in the chase. For as we are permitted to dedicate the horns of stags to the honor of the gods, and to fix the tusks of the boar at our thresholds, so the fruits of the woods are devoted to friendship. Meanwhile, I repudiate the idea that hunting is a business for slaves. Granted that a writer

(Sallust) laid this down who is only to be praised for his style . . . . I prefer you to enjoy country life with Atilius and follow the sport of strength than to be led aside by fair phrases into habits of idleness . . . . Youths should be tested not by the gaming board or ball or attic hoop and Greek Palaestra, but by the ready endurance of fatigue and delight in innocent hardihood.* (The palaestra was a sort of private gymnasium where young men were trained in wrestling or other sports.)

It is known that the Romans were excellent dog trainers, although this first example, from a tale told by Apuleius, ends in disaster.** As mentioned earlier, Roman hunters sometimes blitzed an area. In this case, they had trained their dogs to fan out and surround an area while moving silently. The area was covered with heavy brush, and it was believed that wild goats were hiding in it.

The dogs blocked all exits, then, at a signal, they raised a terrible racket designed to stampede the goats out of the brush and into net traps. But there were no goats in the thicket. Instead an angry wild boar, described as immense, came charging out. Those dogs that attacked were badly torn. And the boar smashed through the net and escaped.

The Romans also trained dogs to do tricks and to perform at the circus and on theater stages as they do today. Plutarch tells of one remarkable dog that performed in the Theater of Marcellus when the Emperor Vespasian was in the audience.

The dog was given food upon which some liquid, presumably poison, had been poured while the audience watched. After eating it, the dog began to shiver and stagger, then it collapsed and apparently died. When some of the actors dragged the body about the stage, the dog gave no sign of life. Then, at some clue from its trainer, who could not be seen by the audience, the dog began to stir. It raised its head, got to its feet, then rushed to fawn at the feet of an actor, presumably its trainer. So clever was the act that the audience thought the dog could have performed it only if he had been given a sleeping potion.

The Romans also hitched the giant dogs of Britain, and probably Irish Hounds too, to carts. Draft dogs have existed in Europe until very recent times because they were cheaper to feed and to house than were horses.

*Symmachus was a 4th Century Roman pagan famed for his epistles, of which the above is a perfect example.
**Lucius Apuleius, Roman Platonicsophist author of *The Golden Ass*, *Metamorphoses*, and *Florida*.

They also could negotiate narrow streets more easily. Cassius Dio Cocceanus* tells of what might have been history's first labor strike and strike breakers. It happened in A.D. 54.

> Such was Nero's general character. I shall now proceed to details. He had such enthusiasm for the horse-races that he actually decorated the famous horses that had passed their prime with the regular street costume of men, and honored them with gifts of money for their feed. Thereupon the horsebreeders and charioteers, encouraged by this enthusiasm on his part proceeded to treat both the praetors and the consuls with great insolence; and Aulus Fabricus, when praetor, finding them unwilling to take part in the contests on reasonable terms, dispensed with their services; and after training dogs to draw chariots, introduced them in place of the horses. At this, the wearers of the White and Red immediately entered their chariots for the races; but as the Greens and Blues would not participate even then, Nero himself furnished the prizes.

The Molossians were said to have come from Epirus in northern Greece, but their true origin is not known. There were two sizes, the larger of which was used as a flock and home guardian. For the former, white was the preferred color. Horace called the Molossians the "shepherd's friendly force." Vergil gave counsel on what to feed them, saying that if properly fed, they would keep off wolves, night robbers, and others. Little or no information is given as to how they were trained.

The Romans believed that dogs possessed certain healing powers. They had noticed that the animals licked clean their wounds and that these usually healed. No doubt, as in some areas today, dogs were allowed to lick the wounds of their masters and particularly those of children.

The Romans believed, too, that the dead lived somewhere deep in the earth, but that the earth also renews itself. Thus, in their complex beliefs, Cerberus, the three-headed dog who guarded the entrance to the kingdom of the dead, played a triple role. He guarded the kingdom, had healing powers, and handled the affairs of the fertility gods.

Roman love of pet dogs is demonstrated best by Martial's famous poem on a little dog, which honors the dog, Issa. The poem shows the noted epigrammatist at his delicate best—a side of his character that was not always present. The opening line of the poem refers to a sparrow that belonged to Lesbia, mistress of the famous poet, Catallus.

*Quoted by Jocelyn Trynta in *Animals in Roman Life and Art.* Cornell University Press, 1973.

83

Issa's more of a rogue than Lesbia's sparrow,
Issa's purer by far than kiss of ring-dove,
Issa's more of a coax than all of the maidens,
Issa's worth all the costly pearls of India,
Issa's Publius' darling lady puppy.
If she whimpers you'll think that she is speaking,
Sorrow and joy she feels as much as he does,
Snuggling close to his neck she sleeps so softly
That you'd scarcely believe the pet was breathing.
If in the night she finds that Nature's calling,
Never a spot she'd leave on master's bedspread.
But with her paw a gentle tap she gives him,
'Please put me down'—and then, 'Please pick me up now."
Modest and chaste a little lap dog is she,
One who knows naught of love, nor could we ever
Find for this tender maid a spouse to match her.
So, lest death should bear off the whole Issa,
Master has had a portrait of her painted
Where you will see so true a likeness of her
That Issa's self is not more truly like her;
Place side by side the real and painted Issas:
Either you'll think that both are living Issas
Or you'll believe that both are in a picture.

It is unfortunate that the painting of Issa has not survived, but we are fortunate to have Martial's poem. For every doting owner of a pet dog can see his own dog in Issa.

A dog whose exact portrait can be seen is one that lived at Pompeii either at the time of the city's destruction or just before. The portrait is painted on a wall frieze in the House of the Epigrams. It is noteworthy that the dog's pasterns have been clipped, as well as the tail, close to the body. The hair of the legs is trimmed to create a bracelet effect. Thus, the "Poodle clips" may have been introduced by the Romans.

Many of the dog breeds mentioned by Xenophon and subsequent writers are little more than names to us, as indeed they were to most of the writers. Some breeds, such as the Molossian, existed in legend as well as in actuality. One breed that was quite famous does not exist in legend, and nothing is known about its origin. This is the Cretan Hound.

One suggestion is that it was a cross between Molossians and Laconians designed to produce a stronger, taller, and more agile dog than the Laconian. It seems more likely to me that it resulted from a cross between Laconians and one of the desert coursing dogs of Egypt. Dogs of the latter type must have been known to the Cretans. And since the Cretan Hounds were used in very rough and mountainous terrain, such a cross would have a chance to suit the needs of the hunters. Some of the Cretan Hounds, if not all of them, had shaggy coats which might indicate a cross with a dog of Afghan type.

A question that always comes up when considering the dogs of Mesopotamia, Greece, and Rome is where did these dogs originate. If from Asia, how did they reach the Mediterranean? And how did they get to Europe?

First, the spread of human population in ancient times is still hotly debated. If there is no agreement on the routes of human migration, there can be none on dogs. But there can be agreement on two points: Dogs accompanied people on their migrations, and dogs were carried by traders over the great trade routes, which existed from prehistoric times.

If, as many suppose, the dog originated in Central Asia, the Himalayas, and Tibet, then traders could have brought dogs from Tibet and over the ancient silk route from Lhasa and Katmandu in Nepal. From there the animals would have moved into India, down the Indus River Valley to the dead city known as Mohenjo Daro, then over water to Bahrain and on to Sumeria. Finally, the great Tibetan Mastiffs would reach Assyria and Babylon.

Evidence suggests that traders were wandering the world as early as 14,500 years ago—the date for the Pelagawra dog of Iraq. Dogs would have travelled with them as well as migrating peoples. From Mesopotamia, dogs would have been taken west to Egypt, Turkey, and Libya; to Crete, Greece, Rome, Syracuse, and Carthage; on to Spain; and south to Ethiopia.

It often is assumed that the modern liking for diminutives shown by the people of China and Japan resulted in the development of the pet and lap dogs. If so, lap dogs could have travelled from Peking (now Beijing), south to Chengdu, then to Lhasa and onward. But there probably was a northern route also—from Xi'an to Turpan, Urumqui, and to Ili; then over the plateaus and valleys to Europe. Such a route, however, would be more likely for large dogs than for lap dogs.

Dogs being taken over the northern route would travel along the great river corridors—along the Volga to Moscow; the Oder, Vistula, and Dvina to the Baltic; and from there to all of Scandinavia. Some would follow the Danube and the Rhine to Germany and France. They might then cross the Pyrenees to the Ebro and move south to all of Spain and Portugal.

Following chapters will explore the dog's presence in western Europe and gradually move farther away from ancient ages and civilizations. In closing this section, one must conclude that the Romans were familiar with most of the families of dogs that have led to today's breeds. Indeed, our breeds are chiefly refinements of dogs they knew.

Horseman and Dog, Sicily, about 510 B.C. Museum of Fine Arts, Boston. Courtesy of William Francis Warden Fund.

11.   *The Celts*

The Greeks called them Keltoi; the Romans often spoke of the land as Gaul. Sometimes they called its inhabitants Celts. A Greek historian who lived between 400 and 330 B.C. wrote a twenty-nine volume history to which his son added another volume. This historian, Ephorus, listed four great groups of barbarians: the Scythians to the north, the Persians to the east, the Libyans in Africa, and the Celts in Europe. Little is known about the Scythians, and much of what the Greeks wrote of them is considered untrue. The Persians were known for their raw power and Indian Hounds; the Libyans were famous for their horses. We know the Libyans had reasonably purebred races of dogs, but that is about all we know—just the breed names.

It is different with the Celts. Before the Roman invasion, they occupied most of western Europe, from Austria to the Atlantic and from the Pyrenees to the British Isles. Though there were a bewildering number of tribes, often making war against each other, they were still so culturally similar, including in language, that all can be called Celts. The people seem to have emerged gradually when the Aegean Civilization began to break up around 1200 B.C. They were well established by 700 B.C., the usual date given for the beginning of the so-called Hallstatt culture in Europe.

Writing in the first century B.C., the Greek historian, Diodorus Siculus reported the following:*

> Physically, the Celts are terrifying in appearance, with deep sounding voices, and very harsh. In conversation, they use few words and speak in puzzles. . . . They have also lyric poets whom they call bards. They sing to the accompaniment of instruments resembling lyres, sometimes a eulogy and sometimes a satire.

*Historical Library, fragment on Caesar's Gallic War. His library contained forty volumes.

That the Celts deserved the epithet "barbarians" cannot be doubted. Indeed, they were said to be "war mad." Lucretius, one of the noblest of the Romans and a peerless thinker and poet, wrote of them in his work, *On the Nature of Things:**

And this race of men from the plains were all the harder, for a hard land had borne them; built on stronger and firmer bones, and endowed with mighty sinews. They were a race undaunted by heat or cold, plague, strange foodstuffs. For many years, among the beasts of the earth, they led their lives. And none was yet a driver of the curved plow, none yet could turn the soil with iron blade, nor bury a new shoot in the ground, nor prune the ripened branch from the tree.

Most people have read about Caesar's conquest of Gaul and how he fragmented the Celts, who, as usual, feuded among themselves. Feeling safe, Caesar moved into Germany and into the British Isles in 55 and 54 B.C. But the Celts rallied to cut him off. In 53 B.C., Caesar attacked Ambiorex, destroying every building, every animal, all food supplies, and most of the people. He wrote that those who survived must surely starve. After taking Avaricum, the Romans slaughtered all but 800 of the 40,000 inhabitants. Vercingetorix rallied the Gauls once more, but Caesar defeated them in 51 B.C. The rule of the Celts in Europe had ended.

Before the conquest by Caesar, the Celtic hordes had invaded Asia Minor, laying waste to much of the area. They finally were contained in Galatia, although they continued to raid and to serve as mercenaries for other peoples. Of some 40,000 people, only about half were fighting men. They did not live in the cities of Galatia, but in their own fortified camps. There they maintained their own language and customs. They were still speaking their native tongue when Saint Paul arrived.

The Celtic rule of Galatia ended in 63 B.C. with the death of Mithridates VI. This man, one of the fabled people of antiquity, became emperor when only eleven, although his mother ruled for him for a time. He was a huge man, a huge eater, a giant in strength, a passionate huntsman, a master of twenty-two languages. He imported poets, artisans, and writers to Galatia and gave them rich prizes. He also gave prizes for the largest eaters.

*Volume 12, Harvard Classics.

88

But there was another side to Mithridates. He trusted no one, and no one in his land was safe. He murdered his mother and his sons. He married his sister, but murdered her also. And then he murdered all the women in his harem. Finally, he had one of his Celt mercenaries kill him.

It was said of the Celts that they were mighty conquerors, poor citizens, always wrangling. But once conquered by the Romans, they were enthusiastic subjects. They produced great bards and developed great poetry that used vivid imagination. After being crushed by Caesar, they never reestablished themselves, except in Ireland, Wales, and the far north of Scotland. The Irish saved the Celtic literature and reintroduced Christianity to Europe. And their ancient Gaelic language is still spoken in the country.

The pre-Roman Celts had two types of hounds, the Segusiae and the Vertragi. The former were named after a tribe, but the origin of the latter is unknown. The Segusiae were trailing hounds; the Vertragi were true coursing dogs of Greyhound type.

As mentioned earlier, the Greek military commander, Arrian, wrote a Cynegeticus. He patterned it after the one written by Xenophon more than five hundred years before, but he added much that Xenophon had omitted or not known. Born in Nicodemia, where he died in 180, Arrian probably wrote his Cynegeticus around 160 while in retirement. Like Xenophon, he seems to have been interested chiefly in hunting. If he knew anything about the dogs that were brought to Rome from Britain and Ireland, it is not evident.

The Segusiae were hunters of hares, and they worked with loud baying. Their cry was even more frenzied when "they own scent." Arrian faulted them, however, because it seemed hard to tell by their baying whether they were on a cold trail or a very hot one. One assumes the frenzied cry came when they were close enough to see the hare.

Arrian wrote that the Segusiae were a rough and sorry-looking lot, and that the very best dogs were also the ugliest. He said that even the Celts likened the hounds to people begging by the roadside. He repeats that they had a pitiful, mournful cry and "give tongue" as if they were furious but still entreating.

Arrian seems to have favored neither the Greek nor the Roman way of hunting hares, finding instead that the truer sport belonged to the Celts. The Greeks often used nets; the Romans liked to blitz an area. But of the Celts he remarks that if they were not hunting for food, they were satisfied if they actually bagged one hare a year.

The Vertragi were true Greyhound-type dogs used for coursing deer. They had slender, pointed muzzles and long, arched necks. Their ears were large, but folded into a half-erect position. Their eyes were prominent and set wide for broader vision. Indeed, after their introduction to the Romans, they often were called "Gaze Hounds." Their eye color, according to Arrian, should be brilliant—black or gray—or "fiery eyed and flashing like lightning." The body was long from head to stern; shoulder blades "stood apart," and the chest was broader than in the modern dog. Their legs were straight, rounded, and compact. The hindquarters were long, meaning, I think, well angulated at the stifle joint. The thighs were heavily muscled, the coat was rough, and the tail somewhat shaggy.

Although Arrian considered it a fault, he did not truly hold heavily overshot (pig jaws) against the dog if it had most other good qualities. He did, however, fault broad necks, thick muzzles, poor eyes, and short bodies. He also discusses temperament at some length. So it seems that poor temperament was a problem then as now.

When Caesar entered Britain, he found that the Celts had huge Mastiff-type dogs plus some smaller ones. Both types shortly showed up in Rome. The former should need no introduction here, except to say that they were heavy-headed, thick of neck, and had huge bodies. While their height is uncertain, it is possible that they were twenty-seven or twenty-eight inches at the shoulder.

The second type of dog has sometimes been called a terrier. Short-legged and heavy-bodied, the dog had a heavy, wedge-shaped head; large upstanding ears; and a curly tail. A bronze figure of such a dog was taken from Coventina's Well, Carrawburgh, Northumberland. It now resides in the Museum of Antiquities at the University of Newcastle, Newcastle-upon-Tyne, England.

The Celts in Ireland had huge dogs that also were taken to Rome, where they created a sensation. They seem to have been the ancestors of the present Irish Wolfhound. The running dog shown in the figure from Moudon, Switzerland, was such a dog.

A number of animals were cult figures in the Celtic religion, including the dog. For example, dogs accompanied the goddess of the forest. Excavations of a Roman temple at Lydney, Gloucester, brought forth a small bronze figure of a dog that also closely resembles the Irish Wolfhound.

It is tempting to say that the so-called War Dogs of Asia, which are shown on the frieze of the Altar of Zeus at Pergamum (or Pergamon), were Celtic. The Celts occupied the land and fought in great battles at Pergamum and elsewhere in Asia Minor.

The dogs on the frieze are huge and extremely muscular. They have very large heads and powerful necks, with a ruff of hair on the lower neck. They have long shaggy tails, but unlike normal Mastiffs, they have upstanding ears. Thus, except for power and size, they are unlike the dogs of Assyria and Babylon, and unlike the dogs from Britain. They may be crosses to British dogs made by the Celts in Asia.

Pretty maiden, Napoleone Elisa Baciocchi, poses with her dog for Sculptor Lorenze Bartolini (1777 - 1850). Courtesy The Cleveland Museum of Art, The Thomas L. Fawick Memorial Collection.

Portion of painting titled BEAR HUNTING IN A WINTER LANDSCAPE. 1861.
Signed by Alfred Wahlberg, artist, and J. W. Wallander. Courtesy National Museum,
Stockholm.

12.

Ancient Britain, Scandinavia, Northern Forests

The primary reason for linking Ancient Britain, Scandinavia, and the northern forests is the need to return to prehistory, to a time when Denmark was part of the European land mass, linked to the east by Sweden and to the west by Britain. The Baltic was a fresh-water lake. Then the shrinking of the ice caps made the seas rise; Britain became isolated, and some of the land of southern Denmark sank.

In 1950, the site of the earliest human settlement ever found in Britain was discovered at Star Carr, Yorkshire. Several canid bones were found at the Star Carr site, which had existed in a period known as preboreal. It was carbon dated at 7538 B.C., plus or minus 350 years. This date roughly corresponds with that of Jericho, where the bones of two dogs were found—one fairly large, the other of about small terrier size.

In a 1954 report, F. C. Fraser (head of the Mammalogy Department at the British Museum) and Dr. J. E. King very carefully suggested that the canid bones found at Star Carr were probably those of a young wolf. But Dr. Magnus Degerbol of the University of Copenhagen made detailed studies of the Star Carr canid, comparing the bones with those of dogs found at Maglemosian sites in Denmark. And he concluded that the Star Carr animal had been a domestic dog.

The Maglemosian culture derives its name from the district where the first settlement sites were found. Star Carr was about a thousand years older than the oldest of these. No one questions that the Maglemosian canids were true dogs. So I think it is worthwhile to give Dr. Degerbol's final conclusion.

I have been able to study the skeletal material from Star Carr and to compare it to the bones of Danish Maglemosian dogs. As a result of this comparison I have come to the conclusion that the said Star Carr canid bones are from a domesticated dog.

93

In a personal communication to me, Cambridge University archaeologists wrote that the animal was a wolf. However, Dr. Degerbol's studies were made with permission from Dr. Fraser, and comparisons such as Dr. Degerbol's have not been made by others. Readers must therefore arrive at their own conclusion.

It is difficult to determine the exact time of changes at the end of the Ice Age. Complications arise because, in the Mesolithic period that followed, people no longer lived in caves. Many lived in pits that were dug in the ground and covered by wood. These have long since disappeared, leaving little by which to trace the people.

The great cave artists were gone by then. But from Sweden to Spain and into North Africa, people continued to paint and engrave pictures of their ways of life. The magnificent works of the cave artists were succeeded by crude "stick" paintings and engravings on rocks. They are stylized, and one might say they are abstractions.

The Mesolithic or middle period lasted in much of Scandinavia from about 8000 to 2000 B.C.; in the far north it extended to 1000 B.C. Most Swedish and Norwegian rock pictures date from about 5000 to 1000 B.C. But about all that can be learned from the paintings, insofar as dogs are concerned, is that the people did have them. It also seems evident that they used dogs for hunting.

Neolithic farmers arrived in Scandinavia about 2500 B.C. An important site for the period is at Lidso, on the island of Lolland, south of Zealand, Denmark. Here, the skeletal remains of eight dogs were excavated. The dogs belonged to a group now commonly called "Turf Dogs," and they appear to have resembled the small Spitz.

Oddly, many of the skulls from Lidso and other sites of the period show fracture marks. It has been suggested by zoologist Dr. Tove Hatting, who studied the fractures, that the dogs' owners may have kicked them or hit them with stones to drive them from the cooking area.

Danish archaeologist Dr. Ulrik Mohl excavated Iron Age sites at Dalshoj and Sorte Muld in Denmark. Dalshoj is dated from 200 B.C. to A.D. 500; Sorte Muld dates from A.D. 200 to 500. This is the time when the dog-horse-human relationship seems to have been formed in Scandinavia. It also would have been the time when dogs from other parts of Europe were moving into the region. The newcomers may have been bred within their racial types or crossed with native dogs.

Some experts speculate that Iron Age hunters rode about on horseback. The horses of the time were small, about the size of present day Icelandic and Welsh ponies. Eventually, the horses grew larger, probably because of better care and feeding and partly because of selective breeding. But hunting by horseback required larger dogs, and indeed they are found during the Iron Age.

The skeletal remains of one Sorte Muld dog indicates that it must have been as large as a modern Great Dane. This would suggest a tremendous change in living conditions. People no longer were always close to starvation. They now seem to have had plenty of food. Hunting had become a recreation as well as a source of food. Only a relatively prosperous culture could have supported dogs of Great Dane size.

But there also is an obvious change in the relationship between people and their dogs, a closer relationship. While the skeletal remains of dogs from the Neolithic Age often showed signs of being kicked, in the Iron Age, dogs were sometimes buried with their masters.

As certain dogs migrated with people to various areas of the world, those with moderate stops and heavy coats moved with their masters into the Northern Forest areas. The Spitz type has been mentioned as an early dog of Scandinavia, but there are many dogs of similar type. Classifiable as Northern Dogs, the group evolved to include the sled dogs of Siberia and the North American Arctic, the Norwegian Elkhound, the Chow Chow, the Japanese Akita, and others.

Except perhaps for the Eskimo's dogs, this is not to say that the distinct breeds known today had been developed. They had not. But the great and dominant Spitz type had become well established. These dogs spread through the Northern Forests, through Finland, Norway, and Sweden, and they were used to hunt elk, bear, and other animals.

It may seem strange to end one period and begin another with the Battle of Agincourt on October 25, 1415. But that battle, plus the earlier ones of Crecy and Poitiers, ended forever the period "When Knighthood Was in Flower."

It was at Agincourt that Edward II, Duke of York, was killed. There, too, Sir Peers Leigh of Lyme Hall, near Stockport, Cheshire, was badly wounded. According to legend, the Mastiff that Sir Peers had brought with him from England guarded his body for hours, until he was taken to Paris, where he died. The bitch was returned to England, where she founded the famous Lyme Hall strain of Mastiffs.

Agincourt spelled the beginning of the end for the feudal system and the rise of a landed gentry. This meant that a hundred times more people could enjoy hunting. They would have the leisure to develop dogs to their

This coat trim suggests that clipping became a style in Roman times for pet dogs, long before it was used for water dogs and Poodles.

Note the similarity of this dog to the dog from the frieze at Pompeii (page 75).

Two types of dogs are shown killing a unicorn in this fifteenth century Swedish picture. Courtesy ATA, Stockholm.

liking and to hunt the type of game they wished. Already Gaston de Foix had written his *Livre de Chasse,* the finest book on hunting since Xenophon. And the finest miniaturists in the world at that time had illustrated it. Now, for dogdom as well as for art, the Renaissance had come.

MOPS. by Carl Gustaf Pilo in 1750. Photo courtesy Statens Konstmusser, Stockholm.

Small bronze dog recovered from Coventina's Well, Carramburgh, Northumberland. Period of Roman Britain. Note resemblance to modern terriers. Courtesy Museum of Antiquities, Newcastle-upon-Tyne, England.

Variety of dogs is shown in this 1670 painting by David Kloker Ehrenstrahl. Swedish National Museum, photo Statens Konstmuseer, Stockholm.

99

Above: Scandinavian Rock Paintings, probably 1500 to 2000 B.C. Dean Harris.

Below: Fourteenth century Scandinavian carving. A goshawk is sent out to blind fast-moving game. The dogs are then tossed, and a huntsman summons the hunters. Note two different types of dogs. Courtesy ATA, Sweden.

100

13.   The Middle Ages of Europe

It is no longer fashionable to call the period between the collapse of the Roman Empire and the dawn of the Renaissance the Dark Ages. It is true that the end of *Pax Romana* in 476 began a period that is characterized as barbaric, feudal, ignorant, and superstitious. But the Middle Ages of the fifth to fifteenth centuries was still a great and eventful time for Europe—indeed, for all the world. And if the first five or six hundred years are still considered Dark Ages, it is not from their lack of achievement, but from our lack of information. For there were no classical writers such as Greece and Rome had known.

Three great Aryan races—the Celts, Teutons, and Slavonians—surged across Europe struggling for supremacy. The Romans had, of course, conquered the Celts in Gaul, Britain, and Spain. Those of Gaul and Spain absorbed the Roman civilization and language, eventually corrupting the latter into what now are called the Romance languages—Italian, French, Spanish, Portuguese, and various dialects. Groups of Celts, speaking their native tongue, existed then, as now, in Ireland, Scotland, and Wales. In these same areas were the few remaining Picts.

The Teutons occupied Denmark, Norway, Sweden, and central Germany. Early Teutonic peoples were among the barbarians who raided the western provinces of the Roman Empire. Some of their tribal names must be remembered, at least dimly, by every former student of high school history. There were the Goths, divided into Visigoths who settled in Spain and Ostrogoths who seized Italy. There were the Burgundians, the Lombards, and the Vandals, who occupied North Africa. The Angles and Saxons took Britain; the Franks captured Gaul, and it was the Herul leader, Odoacer, who overthrew the last Roman emperor of the West, the seven-year-old Romulus Augustulus.

101

The eastern part of the empire largely survived Teutonic invasion and subsequently became known as the Byzantine Empire. With its capital at Constantinople, this empire lasted throughout the thousand-year period, though not without struggles.

Great rulers arose in the West. Clovis forged the Merovingian dynasty, unifying Gaul and becoming King of the Franks. Charles Martel defeated the Saracens and, thus, forever blocked them from Europe. His son Pepin usurped the crown from the Merovingians. And it was Pepin's son Charlemagne, one of history's greatest men, who founded and became emperor of the Holy Roman Empire. The Roman Catholic Church then became the dominant religious power in most of Europe and the British Isles.

The Slavonians settled chiefly in the great eastern plain of European Russia. In addition, there were Magyars in Hungary, the Turks in Anatolia, and the Finns and Laplanders in the far north of Europe. The latter had Mongolian characteristics, at least at that time, and were closely allied to the Chinese.

It is worth remembering that these migrating, conquering peoples had dogs. The dogs must have been crossbred with local breeds, or if they had superior qualities, they may have remained purebred. But this seems doubtful. New territories meant differing conditions, and dog breeders would have bred their animals to adapt to them.

For a thousand years, there was no writer to tell anything about either the dogs of the local people or those of the invaders. Yet there comes an echo from Arrian. No one who has ever listened on a moonless night to an American Foxhound or Coonhound can ever forget his words about the Segusiae and their mournful voices, which were sometimes furious on a hot trail. A coon hunter probably would refer to its "bawl." Thus, the Segusiae seem to be the ancestors of modern Bloodhounds, the various races of Bassets, the Beagles, and Harriers, as well as Foxhounds and Coonhounds.

If there was a period that can legitimately be called the Dark Ages, it ended on Christmas day, 800, when Charlemagne was crowned Emperor of the Holy Roman Empire. Some even say that modern European history begins on that day. But for dogs, the Dark Ages ended approximately in the year 680 with the legend of a wealthy and passionate hunter named Hubert.

Hubert, a pagan, was engaged in what was considered the noblest of all hunting sports—stag hunting. It was Good Friday, and in the deep

102

forest, he encountered a stag. The stag did not flee, and Hubert's dogs would not attack it. Hubert was astounded to see that a crucifix or a cross grew between the horns of the stag. He was instantly converted to Christianity and later became Bishop of Liege.

Bishoprics or Dioceses in those days sometimes covered thousands of acres, and bishops were wealthy people. Hubert had kennels and skilled keepers and trainers, probably in various parts of his bishopric. And his hounds were legendary for their ability.

Hubert died in 727, and later was canonized. His dogs, eventually called Saint Hubert's Hounds, spread across the regions that became France, Belgium, Germany, and the British Isles. Thus, it is fair to think that the Segusiae and Saint Hubert's Hounds were the foundation stock for all the breeds just mentioned, and probably also the Dachshund.

Much of what is known about dogs of the past has come from writers who gloried in hunting and who, in the main, described hunting dogs. But other breeds also seem to have reached Europe after the collapse of the Roman Empire, during the early part of the Middle Ages. These were giant guard-dog breeds, perhaps some coursing dogs, and some dogs for hunting small game. They probably entered the region with the Huns.

Historians and ethnologists list four races of people who have been termed the Huns. The Chinese called them the Hiung-Nu, which seems to have been a generalized term for warring nomadic tribes. These are the Huns who, under Attila and others, ravaged the Roman Empire between 372 and 453. A second group was made up of those called the Magyars. They entered Hungary in 898, and from them have evolved most of the people now classed as Hungarians. A third group, called the White Huns or Ephthalites, invaded Persia. The fourth, the Hunas, invaded India. The Bulgars may have been offshoots of Attila's Huns.

During the first century after Christ, the Chinese began forcing the Hiung-Nu westward. The Magyars seem to have stopped first at the Don, then eventually to have crossed the Carpathians into Hungary. Attila's Huns had their base in the southern Urals, where some may have returned after scourging Rome. Another division stopped in Afghanistan. The Bulgars may have belonged to this group, as may have the Turks, although they were not called Turks before the fifth century.

The Huns were superb horsemen who loved the chase. Since one tribe stopped at Afghanistan, it is possible that from their coursing dogs came the long-coated ancestors of the Afghan. It also seems probable that the Steppe Greyhound, one of the ancestors of the Russian Wolfhound or

Borzoi, came from their dogs. And it is tempting to suppose that the Huns used smaller dogs to hunt small game, and that the Vizsla came from these. But since this dog is so close in type to other pointing breeds, it is more likely that crosses were made with European Pointers.

As with other migrating peoples, these nomadic warriors moved with their families and their flocks. Sheep-sized dogs guarded the flocks, and they had the general characteristics of the dogs that now are associated with Tibet. Many other breeds known today came from the dogs of the Huns. From Hungary came the Komondor, Kuvasz, and Puli. The Ovcharkas came from European Russia, the Maremma from Italy, the Shar Planinetz from Yugoslavia. And from Turkey came the Anatolian Shepherd Dog.

It probably is incorrect to suppose these animals were purebred for a thousand years. But they did form races with dominant characteristics of size, guarding instincts, trainability, coat type, and so on. However, Switzerland poses a problem.

An Alpine country, Switzerland has been called "the turntable of Europe" because of its mountain passes that lead into Germany, Italy, and France. Among them are the Simplon and the Saint Bernard. These passes permitted travel by traders and by warriors such as the Huns.

There is a culture in Switzerland called Egolzwil that dates back to 2900 B.C. It is estimated that its first farmers arrived about 200 years after this date. The bones of domestic animals have been found in Egolzwil sites, but not those of dogs. Archaeologists wonder if this is purely an accident of history, or if the dog had not yet arrived in that area.

Now 2700 B.C. is relatively late in the prehistory of dogs. Additionally, those early farmers had cereal grains, and these must have come from the southeast where dogs were well known. It is generally considered that the large shepherd dogs of the Huns came from the southeast, and that some of them travelled the Alpine passes into Italy, France, and Germany. We also suppose that the Huns left behind some of their great shepherd dogs, and that these could be the ancestors of the Swiss mountain dogs. Alpine conditions would be similar to those in Tibet, the original home of the giant dogs.

The Celts and the Helvetii had occupied Gaul and Switzerland. They were not noted as farmers or stock growers but as warriors. The Romans conquered Switzerland around 58 B.C. Now the great mountain passes, as I have pointed out, led into the fertile valleys to the West. But they also were two-way corridors.

The problem is this: Did the great dogs of the Alpine mountains arrive with or after the Romans? Were they brought from the West by farmers and stock growers who were searching for the fertile valleys of Switzerland, where they would be out of the way of European warriors? The answer belongs to the Dark Ages of dogdom.

It was during the Middle Ages that the feudal system reached its height in Europe. Reduced to its simplest terms, the feudal system was one in which the peasants relied upon powerful barons, counts, and kings for protection during the nearly constant wars that raged across Europe and the British Isles.

The powerful lords enlisted the services of knights. The knights were men of "gentle" and even noble birth, who excelled at fighting. They fought on horseback or, if unhorsed, on the ground, while encased in heavy armor. Some had their own estates; others simply depended upon the barons for food and lodging. There was, in addition, a service class— the merchants, armorers, physicians, etc. In many cases, the peasants did not live on the land they farmed. They simply rented the land from the lords, paying in portions of the crops they raised.

Throughout history dogs had been owned by the rich and powerful, and dog breeding and the development of races of dogs had been in their hands. The question is often raised: Did the peasants have dogs? Except for shepherd dogs, there is no complete answer. But there are hints in the Dark Ages which give us some indication of breed names.

Howel Dda became Prince of Deheubarth in south central Wales in 943. He summoned jurists from all over his princedom, and had the laws codified. Bleggwryd, archdeacon of Llandall, is said to have taken them down. Howel lists two classifications of dogs. The first class is that of "Dogs of high value." They are the Tracker, Greyhound, Spaniel, Bloodhound, Covert Hound, and Harrier. In the second class are "Dogs of lower rank"—the Mastiff (cur), Shepherd's Dog, and House Dog (cur).

Now tradition has it that William the Conqueror introduced Bloodhounds to England after he had defeated Harold at Hastings in 1066. Yet Howel had mentioned the breed by name more than a hundred years before that time. Howel also mentions Greyhounds by name. William the Conqueror supposedly passed a law making Bloodhounds the sole property of gentlemen, so that the term Blooded Hounds became popular. Also that only men with titles (degrees) could own Greyhounds. And thus "degreehounds" eventually shortened to Greyhounds.

Obviously neither explanation can be correct. The first mention of the spaniel is made by Howel, he believing as has everyone since, that the spaniels came from Spain.

I think we get one clue about the Mastiffs of the Middle Ages from Howel. He labels them as "curs." And this could mean that the Mastiff in those days was simply a giant dog which could be used for a variety of purposes. House pets, too, were listed as curs. Thus, "cur" could mean any small mongrel dog kept in the home.

Canute was king of Norway, Denmark, and England from 995 until his death in 1015. His was a relatively peaceful reign. During it he had time to codify many of the laws in his dominions. Some of them deal with dogs and supply us with some indications as to the position of the peasants. The crown lands were vast and supplied the king and his courtiers with much hunting pleasure. The penalty for unauthorized hunting on crown lands ranged from death to putting out the eyes of the offender, and very heavy fines. People could, and did, live in the forests. They could own small house pets, but were forbidden to hunt or trap. Dogs of medium to large size were lamed, usually by cutting the tendons at the hock joint. Few people wanted to pay such a price to own a dog.

Earlier I have given two dates for the ending of the "Dark Ages"—680 for the conversion of Saint Hubert, and the founding of the Saint Hubert line of Bloodhounds, and 800, the day Charlemagne was crowned head of the Holy Roman Empire. But the end of the feudal system began at the Battle of Agincourt on October 25, 1415. The small, invading English army faced a mighty French force. Torrential rains had slowed the advance of the English for several days, and continued when the two armies met. The French knights charged, but their horses were bogged down in the mud. English crossbowmen slaughtered them. Unhorsed, the knights could not move well in their heavy armor. They, too, were slaughtered. The French constable, five thousand nobles, three dukes, five counts, and ninety barons, plus some fifteen hundred "men of gentle blood" were killed. The English lost thirteen men at arms and one hundred foot soldiers.

The use of professional knights in armor was ended forever. The feudal system, which had supported them, was also dying. So was the exclusive right of the nobles to hunt and to own hunting dogs. And it followed that a growing number of comparatively wealthy middle class people could develop the art of hunting to its present perfection. And to do this, they also developed the great variety of dog breeds we now know.

106

Moreover, the great variety of non-hunting dogs could also be developed. Dog breeding and competition with dogs became a hobby well within the financial reach of millions of people.

Agincourt has one more connection with the modern dog. Sir Peers Leigh of Lyme Hall, Stockport, Cheshire, fell mortally wounded in the battle. A Mastiff bitch stood over him, guarding the wounded man until English soldiers found him. He was taken to Paris, where he died. In the meantime, the Mastiff had given birth to eight pups. She and her puppies were shipped to Lyme Hall, along with the body of Sir Peers. It is assumed that the bitch had accompanied Sir Peers to France, but history is not clear on this. Dogs were sometimes used as armor bearers, but it seems unlikely that a bitch heavy in whelp would be taken along for any reason. At any rate, she and her pups became foundation stock for one of the most famous kennels in the world. Lyme Hall Mastiffs are still in demand in Great Britain, where the breed is called the Old English Mastiff.

In the fourteenth century, the great plagues known as the Black Death spread across Europe, killing an estimated 25,000,000 people. There were two types of plague, bubonic and pneumonic, and both were spread by fleas. There are some five hundred species of fleas, but those of particular interest here are the nearly extinct human flea, dog and cat fleas, and rat and mouse fleas.

In the Middle Ages almost all people—kings, nobles, fair ladies, and peasants—were unwelcome hosts to human fleas. But these do not appear to have been vectors of either type of plague, nor do the dog and cat fleas. Either the plague vectors could not live on dogs and cats, or the dogs and cats were immune to the infecting agent. Had this not been the case, the close communal relationship of dogs would have brought their total decimation. And nothing like this occurred. (It should be noted that in the American far west, there is a flea which lives on wildlife, chiefly the squirrel, which can be a vector of bubonic plague.)

North Africa of the Middle Ages presents a differing yet in some ways similar picture. For a time, Christianity protected itself by moving its headquarters from Rome to what became Constantinople. Later, the rise of Islam caused its return to Rome. But Islam became the protector of the arts—architecture, literature, painting. The early Greek and Roman influences largely disappeared, except in the matter of dogs and sport.

The wealthy had their hounds for the chase, and gazelles were plentiful. So different areas developed their own coursing dogs. They were of Saluki or Greyhound type and they had locally derived names, albeit similar to Saluki. Also, there were giant dogs of Mastiff type.

North African shepherds faced different problems from those of Europe. The predators they faced were hyenas, jackals, lions, and in some areas, leopards. They solved this with sheep guarding dogs which are among the greatest in the world. The general name for them is Anatolian, with some being registered in the "West" as Karabash and Akbash.

We know nothing about the dogs of the lower classes, if there were any. In general the Islamic religion had great contempt for dogs. The poverty of the peasants also tended to prevent dog ownership. Some communities were walled for protection from jackals and hyenas, and some few had giant dogs which served as protectors for the community. A general Islamic prohibition against killing dogs meant that great numbers of sick and aged dogs were deserted. They formed a large canine community of pariahs. To survive, these homeless animals had to be superior in intelligence and stamina, and it is from this group that the current Israeli breed, known as the Canaan Dog, originates. Presently, it is gaining some popularity in the United States and Canada.

Modern Guard Dog. Shar Planinetz guarding sheep on migration. Photo by Dr. Ray Coppinger, head of the Guard Dog Project, Hampshire College.

14.   The European Renaissance

In beginning this chapter on the European Renaissance, several points should be made clear. First, the Middle Ages had not been dead. By the time the Renaissance began, the major races of dogs had been developed and were well established all over Europe, as far north as the Arctic. From these races would come the refined breeds, but the basic families existed.

Second, it must be remembered that only in relatively recent times were dogs divided into hounds and dogs. Previously, any dog might be called a hound, whereas today we would restrict the term to the trailing and sight hunting, or coursing, breeds. Occasionally, the distinction still is not made. Thus, the Scandinavian and Dutch *hund* and *hond* have been translated into hound, as in Norwegian Elkhound and Keeshond.

The third point concerns paintings. Artists did not cease to function after the Roman Empire collapsed. Still, it used to puzzle me that the Medieval artists portrayed the fully clothed human so excellently, but painted the nude human in thoroughly unreal and ugly fashion. And yet their cows were shown to perfection. Renaissance artists were only slightly more successful.

I now know there was a reason. The artists were obsessed with mathematics and, by using mathematics, with trying to recreate the internal rhythm of the great Greek sculptures. They always failed. Both Leonardo da Vinci and Albrecht Durer failed when they tried it. Measurements of the various parts of the human body could not be put together to form a true portrait. But no one had bothered to measure animals. So the art teachers simply instructed their students to draw their animals naturally. They did, and the results were great.

109

DIANA AND HER NYMPHS DEPARTING FOR THE CHASE, by Peter Paul
Rubens, 1577-1640. The Cleveland Museum of Art. Leonard C. Hanna, Jr. Bequest.

110

The Ladies Amabel and Mary Jemima Yorke, by Sir Joshua Reynolds, 1723-1792. The Cleveland Museum of Art. Bequest of John L. Severance, 1936.

Self Portrait of William Hogarth (1697-1764) and his Pug, painted in 1745. Courtesy of The
Tate Gallery, London.

Coat trim on this pet dog painted by Pieter Van Slingelandt (1640-1691) shows that the so-called "Poodle Trim" did not begin with water-retrieving dogs, but simply as a style. Courtesy Staatliche Kinstsammlungen, Dresden.

Diana with Greyhound, Garden at Versailles. Photo by Riddle.

114

Diana with Scent Hound, Garden at Versailles. Photo by Riddle.

This is important for a special reason. One could never be certain that the Egyptians were not idealizing their dogs, stylizing them, or making abstractions. But the great Renaissance artists were painting true pictures of living dogs. And so we can believe what is seen.

After nearly one thousand years of silence on the subject of dogs, a French count, Gaston de Foix, wrote one of the finest texts on hunting ever produced. It was called, in short, the *Livre de Chasse,* or *Book of the Chase.* The book was started on May 1, 1387, and since the count died four years later, it must have been written in the intervening years.

De Foix was a great patron of the arts, and French artists had developed the painting of miniatures to its highest point at that time in Europe. De Foix commissioned artists to illustrate his manuscript with eighty remarkable color plates. I have seen some of them in the Bibliotheque Nationale in Paris and all eighty in black-and-white reproduction.

Gaston de Foix wrote in an antique idiomatic French, which kept the book from being published except in manuscript copies. But Edward II, Duke of York, translated de Foix's work into the English of his time. He added some chapters of his own, left out de Foix's chapters on trapping and snaring, then claimed authorship of the entire work. He named his book *The Master of Game.*

Although nineteen manuscript copies were made, *The Master of Game* was not published in book form until 1899. Then publishers William A. and F. Baillie-Grohman modernized the text insofar as was possible without destroying the charm and character of the language Edward used. They published a limited, beautifully illuminated edition. In 1904, they brought out a less expensive edition, for which President Theodore Roosevelt wrote the foreword.

But first, about Gaston de Foix. He was called Gaston Phoebus because he was as handsome as a golden-haired god. A feudal lord, he held a large territory of Foix and Bearn along the Spanish border. He had knights in attendance, men at arms, servants, peasant farmers, and merchants, and all owed loyalty to him. He also had stables and kennels in various sections of his estates, as well as grooms and trainers. His kennels may have had one hundred or more dogs.

De Foix was one of the great statesmen of his time. Although importuned by both sides, he managed to remain neutral in the wars that raged between England and France. He is, however, said to have murdered his son. And when a neighboring province was infested with robbers and forest bandits, its people petitioned de Foix for help. He responded by rounding up four hundred lawbreakers and executing them in a single day, some by drowning. He won the praise of the entire area.

Edward II, Duke of York, is the terrible villain of Shakespeare's *Richard the Second.* He was very much the villain in real life as well, even considering the time in which he lived. History charges him with complicity in the murder of Gloucester. He carried the head of his brother-in-law on a pike through the streets. And he joined his sister in an attempt to assassinate the king and to carry off the Mortimer brothers, one of whom was heir presumptive to the throne of England.

For the latter offense, Edward was imprisoned in Pevensey Castle between 1406 and 1413. During that time, he translated de Foix's *Chasse.* It is believed that Edward, who had once been governor of Aquataine, may have known de Foix. Both men were masters in their knowledge of dogs, wild animals, and hunting. Edward died at the Battle of Agincourt, described earlier.

President Roosevelt's foreword in the 1904 edition of *The Master of Game* pointed out that hunting not only was a passion but also a disease of the era's nobility. Even Louis XVI of France wrote in his diary that a day in which he did not kill game was a blank day for him.

Louis XVI was a drive-up gunner—that is, he took a station, and drivers forced the game to run or fly past him. (De Foix and the Duke of York considered this effeminate.) The king was engaged in such a hunt when the Paris mob seized him and Marie Antoinette.

Jean Froissart, a French priest to whom de Foix gave a church, was the great chronicler of his time. Froissart enjoyed wine and gossip and visited the important people of France and England to get information for his chronicles. Much of what is known about de Foix's personal life comes from Froissart. He probably got the following account of de Foix's death from the count's favorite knight and companion, Sir Espang de Lyon, who was present.

On the day that he died, he had hunted and killed a boar, and by that time it was high noon. He rode to dinner at the hospital of Rions, where he alighted and went into his chamber, which was strewed with green herbs, and the walls set full of green bows to refresh the chamber, for the air without was excessively hot, being in the month of May (one text says August).

When he felt the fresh air, he said: "This freshness does me much good, for the weather has been very hot"; and so sat down in a chair, and conversed with Sir Espang de Lyon of his hounds, which had run best.

As the earl washed his hands before dinner, suddenly his heart failed him, and he fell down, and when he fell he said: "Ah, I am but dead. God have mercy upon me." He spoke not a word after . . . and in less than half an hour he gently yielded up his breath and died without a struggle. God of his pity have mercy upon him.

When the news of the earl's death reached Orthez,
. . . every man, woman, and child cried and wept piteously . . . in remembrance of his nobleness and puissant estate, his bravery and generosity, and the great prosperity that he lived in; for there was neither French nor English that durst displease him.

Gnossis, the earliest of the known Greek mosaicists, made a mosaic showing two naked swordsmen killing a stag. It was extremely dangerous to approach a stag at bay, so most hunters dispatched it from a safe distance. To kill it with a sword, or to "spay" it, required extreme courage and great skill. The following quote of de Foix, as translated by Edward II, includes the two authors' differing words in brackets.

The best sport that men can have is running with hounds, for if he hunt at hare, or at the roe or buck, or at the hart, or any other beast (without Greyhound—Edward) (or if one hunts stags, drawing from them without having first harboured them with a lymer—de Foix) it is a fair thing, and pleasant to him that loveth them; the seeking and the finding is also a fair thing, and a great liking to slay them with strength, and for to see the wit and the knowledge that God hath given to good hounds, and for to see good recovering and retrieving, and the mastery and subtleties that be in good hounds.

For with Greyhounds, the sport lasteth not, for anon a good Greyhound or a good Alaunte taketh or faileth a beast, and so do all manner of hounds save running hounds, the which must hunt all day, questeying and making great melody in their language and saying great villainy and chiding the beasts that they chase. And therefore I prefer them to all other kinds of hounds, for they have more virtue, it seems to me, than any other beast. (De Foix mentions that some small hounds are called kents and large ones, harriers.)

One of the dogs mentioned by de Foix was the lymer. This was a tracking hound led by a groom. The dogs were taught the difference between the track and scent of a hart (male), a hind (female), and a young deer. Lymers were heavy-bodied, with large heads and droop ears, though not as long as those of a modern Bloodhound. One variety was a reddish brown color. The tails of all Lymers had a slight saber curve.

Raches appear to have been smaller running hounds used chiefly on hare, perhaps sometimes on fox. Small Greyhounds, rather than Raches, were used for badger drawing. What de Foix had to say about the gray badger is, because of its quaintness and the old wives tale it includes, worth mentioning.

Once a year they farrow their pigs in their burrows as does the fox. When they be hunted they defend themselves long and mightily and have evil biting and venomous as the fox, and yet they defend themselves better than the fox. It is the beast of the world that gathereth most grease within, and that is because of the long sleeping that he sleepeth. And his grease bears medicine as does that of the fox, and yet more, and men say that if a child that hath never worn shoes is first shod with those made of the skin of the grey, that child will heal a horse of farcy (glanders) if he should ride upon him, but thereof I have no affirmation.

De Foix and Edward II were thoroughly familiar with spaniels. Both said the breed got its name from its country of origin "notwithstanding that there are many in other countries." They were used to quarter their ground and to "start fowl or beasts."

But their right craft is of the partridge and the quail. It is a good thing to a man that hath of a noble goshawk, or a tiercel, or a sparrow hawk for partridge to have such hounds. And also when they be taught to be couchers (setters) they be good to take partridge and quail with the net.

There were, it seems, three kinds of alauntes. The alaunte gentle, the alaunte veutreres, and the alaunte butcheries. De Foix says that, like the spaniels, they came from Spain. He did not much care for the alaunte gentle. They were shaped like a Greyhound, though fuller bodied and with a larger head, and de Foix thought they should be better trained.

Also, they run at oxen and sheep, and swine, and at all other beasts, or at men, or at other hounds. For men have seen alauntes slay their masters. In all manner of ways alauntes are treacherous and evil understanding, and more foolish and more harebrained than any other kind of hound . . . .

One wonders why they were called alauntes gentle. Yet he also praises them.

For a good alaunte should run as fast as a Greyhound, and any beast that he can catch he should hold with his seizers and not leave it. For an alaunte of his nature holds faster of his biting than can three Greyhounds the best any man can find.

That other kind of alaunte is called veutreres. They are almost shaped as a Greyhound of full shape, they have a great head, great lips, and great ears, and with such men help themselves at the baiting of the bull and at hunting the wild boar.

That other kind of alauntes of the butcheries is such as you may always see in good towns, that are called great butchers' hounds, the which the butchers keep to help to bring their beasts that they buy in the country . . . . Also they keep their master's house, they be good for bull baiting and for the wild boar . . . . They cost little to keep for they eat the foul things in the butchers' row.

Both writers mentioned dogs for bull baiting. It seems obvious that these were in no respect like the traditional Bulldogs of the past and certainly unlike those of the present. About the only similarity is that the original bull baiters had great courage, grabbed with their "seizers," and hung on.

Always in trying to trace the origin of dogs—and people—there are unanswerable puzzles. One lies in the legend of Saint Hubert, which is known to have been ascribed to him after his death. Hubert then became the patron saint of hunters. But there also was an earlier patron saint, a Roman nobleman who, after seeing the stag and crucifix, was converted to Christianity. He became Saint Eustace. Both de Foix and Edward II list a variety of trailing hounds. Although tradition holds that many trailing hounds descend from those of Saint Hubert, neither author mentions Saint Hubert or his hounds.

Modern writers use the word hound to describe dogs that trail or that hunt by sight, such as Bloodhound or Greyhound. A Mastiff, for instance, would not be called a hound. However, as mentioned before, in Europe the Dutch *hond* is dog, and the Scandinavian *hund* is dog. In the United States, The American Kennel Club has mistranslated these, thereby deriving the names Elkhound and Keeshond. With this explanation, de Foix's description is quoted.

> The Mastiff is a manner of hound. The Mastiff's nature and his office is to keep his master's beasts and his master's house, and it is a good kind of hound, for they keep and defend with all their power all their master's goods. They be of a churlish nature and ugly shape . . . . Also of Mastiffs and Alauntes, there be bred hounds that are good for the wild boar.

De Foix's quaint but apt descriptions of the Greyhound's head and rear end are worth repeating.

> A Greyhound should have a long head and somewhat large made, resembling the making of a brace (pike). A good large mouth and good seizers, the one against the other, so that the nether jaw pass not the upper, nor that the upper pass not the nether.

And of the rear end, he writes,

> . . . a little pintel (penis) and little ballocks, and well trussed near the ars, small womb, and straight near the back like a lamprey, the thighs great and straight as a hare, the hocks straight and not bent as an ox, a cat's tail making a ring at the end.

Dr. Caius on English Dogs

Dr. Johannes Caius (1510-1573) was physician to King Edward VI of England. His real name was probably John Kay or Key; but during his time, names were often given in their Latin form because that language was considered the only permanent one. All educated men were taught Latin, and any work designed to be permanent was written in the language. In this way, educated men of whatever nationality could converse. In 1570, almost two hundred years after de Foix, Dr. Caius wrote his famous treatise, *Of Englishe Dogges*. He wrote it to his friend, the noted Swiss naturalist, Conrad Gesner.

Dr. Caius's treatise is the first to mention terriers as such. It is well to remember that the British do not consider dogs terriers unless they have been developed in the British Isles or have descended from dogs that were. Terriers of other national extraction, such as the Miniature Schnauzer, are not classified as such in England. Here is what Caius wrote about terriers.

There are hounds that will hunt fox and hare alternately, but not with the same luck as when following their natural bent, for they often go wrong. Some are fox and some badger hounds only: called Terrarii because they penetrate holes in the earth, as ferrets do when after rabbits, and so frighten and bite the fox and the badger that they either tear them on the ground with their teeth, or force them from their lairs into flight, or into nets drawn over the burrows. These are the smallest class of Sagaces.

Caius listed one breed as Sanguinarii, or Bloodhound, and his description of it will last for all time. Indeed, the Bloodhounds of his time were little different from those of today in conformation and performance. Here is what he said about them.

The larger class remain to be mentioned: These, too, have drooping lips and ears, and it is well known that they follow their prey not only while alive but also after death when they have caught the scent of blood. For whether the beasts are wounded alive and slip out of the hunter's hands, or are taken dead out of the warren (but with profusion of blood in either case) these hounds perceive it at once by smell and follow the trail. For that reason they are properly called Sanguinarii.

Frequently, however, an animal is stolen, and owing to the cleverness of the thieves there is no effusion of blood; but even so they are clever enough to follow dry human footsteps for a huge distance, and can pick a man out of a crowd however large, pressing on through the densest thickets, and they will still go on even though they have to swim across a river. When they arrive at the opposite bank, by a circular movement, they find out which way a man has gone, even if at first they do not hit on the track of the thief. Thus they supplement good luck by artifice and deserve what Aelian (Italian, third century, A.D.) says of them in C-59 of his Historia Animalium, where he argues that these dogs can think and reason, and come to a decision; nor do they cease to follow until the thieves have been caught.

During the day their masters keep them in darkness, and bring them out at night, the idea being that if they are used to the dark, they will be all the quicker in tracking robbers, who above all things are fond of the dark. When these dogs hunt thieves, they are not given the same liberty as when after beasts, unless they flee at great speed, but they are held back in the leash and so guide their master, on foot or horseback, at such speed as suits him.

On the Anglo-Scottish border, because of frequent cattle and horse raids, much use is made of these dogs, and they learn to follow animals first and to chase thieves later and as a secondary occupation.

Caius is the first author to mention otter hounds. He said they have a natural instinct for working in water, whereas other breeds only enter the water because of a strong desire to catch the prey. And bitches, he said, are called Brach or, by the Scotch, Rachs.

Caius referred to another group, *Canis Generosus,* and listed one member, the Maltese, which he called Pachyni. (The Romans had called it Melitei.) Now Caius was a sufficiently great physician to be the king's own, which makes what he said about the Maltese all the more interesting.

This is a tiny breed of dog, and only sought after to be a luxurious plaything for women. The smaller it is the more welcome is it, for that purpose and for being carried in the bosom in the bedchambers, or in their hands when driving out. It is no use at all except that it will relieve indigestion if pressed against the stomach or moved up and down the breast of a sick person, because of the difference in temperature. Nay, it is even believed that diseases will pass, through the sickness and also the death of these: as though the evil passed into them because of the similarity of heat.

123

Two dogs that Caius listed in the Rusticus Class deserve mention—the Shepherd Dog and the Molossian. He said that in England (and presumably Scotland) shepherds followed their sheep; on the other hand, in France, Germany, Syria, and Tartary, shepherds lead their sheep. The reason he gave is that in England there are no wolves. (King Edgar, about A.D. 959, required an annual tribute to King Lud of Cambria of three thousand wolves. Since that time, Britain has been free of wolves.) This is the description Caius gave of the forerunners of today's Collies and Border Collies, and Old English and Shetland Sheepdogs.

But as to this dog. If his master utters a certain command, or a clear whistle through his closed fist, he will drive all stray sheep into one place, and this the one the master wants; so that with no real trouble and without even stirring the shepherd can govern the whole flock as he likes, making them advance or halt or retreat or move to and fro. And I have carefully made this observation when travelling, and noticed people curbing their horses by the shepherd's whistle, so that one can visually test the truth of the fact. With this same dog, the shepherd can get hold of a sheep to kill or to cure, without doing any injury to it.

Caius called the Molossian Villatic, saying it "is big and robust. Its body has great weight, but little speed. To look at it is, however, terrible, and so is its voice." It was used to protect farms from thieves, to fight wild boars, and even to bait bulls and control them. "For the breed is most bellicose and violent; and a danger even to men, for they do not fear men. Nor does war terrify them."

Molossians were chained to the door during the day "for fear of harm if it were loose." Some were used by butchers; others carried letters fastened to their collar. Still others, used by traveling merchants, carried goods in pack saddles. Some which Caius called Lunarius, served as night guards since, sleepless, they bayed at the moon. And others, called Aquarii, were larger and "will pump water out of deep wells for use in the country by pulling a long rope."

Germany, Northern Europe, Sweden

Sweden's Carl von Linne (1707-1778) is one of the immortals of natural history. More commonly known as Linnaeus, he developed the classification system of plants and animals that is named after him.

124

Linnaeus's classification of dogs is of no use today, but he did make some highly interesting notes on dogs in general, as well as specific notes on breeds known in Sweden. He also listed a few South American breeds, although some people doubt their actual existence.

The dog . . . is the enemy of all beggars, and often attacks strangers without any provocation; will lick wounds, and often by so doing relieves ulcers and the gout; howls at certain notes in music, and sometimes urines on hearing them; bites a stone when flung at it; grows sick at the approach of storms . . . makes a violent following when Empyreumatic oils are rubbed on the tail (empyr refers to flame) . . . is often infected with gonorrhea . . . is the victim of anatomists for demonstrating the circulation of the blood, the lacteal vessels, and for experiments on transfusion, cutting of nerves, and other cruel purposes; but has been made a useful martyr by some, for discovering the effects of remedies against poison.

The following list from Linnaeus's notes omits those breeds already covered, except for an occasional note of help or interest. Also omitted are the Latin names given by him.

Shepherd's Dog. Has erect ears, the tail is wooly underneath.
Pomeranian Dog. Has long hairs on the head, erect ears, and the tail is much curved upwards on the rump.
Siberian Dog. Has erect ears, a curled up tail, and the hair on the whole body is long.
Iceland Dog. The ears are erect, with pendulous points; and the hair is universally long, except on the snout which is short.
Great Water Dog. The hair is long and curled like the fleece of a sheep.
Lesser Water Dog. Is of a small size with long curly hair, which about the ears is longer and hangs downward.
Pyrame. Has a small rounded head, with short snout, and the tail is turned up on the back.
Shock Dog. Is about the size of a squirrel, having very long, soft, silky hair all over the body.
Lion Dog. Is exceedingly small, with long hair, like the foregoing, on the fore part of the body; that on the hind parts being shorter and smooth.

Little Danish Dog. Has small, half pendulous ears, a small pointed nose, and thin legs.

Bastard Pug Dog. Has small, half pendulous ears, and thick flattish nose.

Pug Dog. The nose is crooked upward, the ears are pendulous, and the body is square built.

This variety has a resemblance to the bull-dog, but it is much smaller and entirely wants his savage ferocity. Of this there are two sub-varieties, Viz:

(a) The Artois dog of Buffon, produced between the pug-dog and the bastard pug-dog.

(b) The Alicant dog of Buffon, produced between the pug-dog and the spaniel.

Bulldog. Is as large as a wolf having the sides of the lips very pendulous, and the body very strong and robust. The nose of this variety is short, and the under jaw is longer than the upper; this kind is exceedingly fierce and cruel, attacks without warning, but with little judgment and never quits its hold. It is peculiar to England for baiting bulls, which practice, and consequently the kind of dog, is now much less frequent than formerly. There are several varieties of this in size and colour.

Mastiff . . . . This dog is peculiar to England . . . . Some will permit a stranger to come into the yard or place which he has been appointed to guard, and will go peaceably along with him through every part of it, so long as he touches nothing; but the moment he attempts to meddle . . . he informs him with gentle growling . . . and never uses violence unless resisted; and will even in this case, seize the person, throw him down, and hold him there for hours, or until relieved, without biting.

German Hound. Has pendulous ears, and a spurious toe, usually called a dew-claw, on each hind foot.

Hound. Is of a whitish ground colour; has pendulous ears, and dew-claws on each hind foot.

Pointer. The tail is short, and has the appearance of having been cut.

Barbet (a type of Poodle). The tail is truncated, or seems cut off in the middle, with long coarse hair.

Irish Greyhound. Is of the size of a Mastiff, with an arched body and narrow snout; and having the fur somewhat curled.

Rough Greyhound. Same size body and snout as the Common Greyhound, but having the hair somewhat longer and curled.

126

Italian Greyhound. Of small size, but the same form of body and snout as the Common Greyhound.

Oriental Greyhound. Tall, slender, with very pendulous ears, and very long hairs on the tail, hanging down a great length.

Naked Dog. Has no hair on the body.

Lurcher. The body is narrow, and covered with short, thickset hair; the legs are long and the tail is thick and straight.

Rough Lurcher. In body, legs and tail, resembles the last, but is covered with long, harsh hair.

Boar Lurcher. The head and snout are strongly made; the hind part of the body is lank; the legs are long, and the hair is long and harsh.

Turnspit. Has short legs and a long body, which is mostly spotted. (a) With straight legs. (b) With crooked legs. (c) With long shaggy hair.

Alco. About the size of a squirrel, having a small head, pendulous ears, a curved body and short tail. Of this animal, there are two kinds mentioned by authors.

Fat Alco. Is prodigiously fat; the head is very small, and the ears are pendulous; the fore part of the head is white, and the ears yellowish. The neck is short; the back is arched, and covered with yellow hair; the tail is white, short and pendulous; the belly is large, and spotted with black, the legs and feet are white. The female has six conspicuous paps.

Techichi. Is like the small dogs of Europe, but has a wild melancholy air.

New Holland Dog. (The Dingo?) The tail is bushy and hangs downwards; the ears are short and erect, and the muzzle is pointed. Inhabits New Holland (early name for Australia). This animal is rather less than 2 feet high, and about 2 feet and a half in length. His head resembles that of a fox, having a pointed muzzle, garnished with whiskers, and short erect ears; the whole body and tail is of a light brown colour, growing paler towards the belly, on the sides of the face, and on the throat; the hind parts of the fore legs, the fore parts of the hind legs and all the feet are white. On the whole, it is a very elegant animal, but fierce and cruel; and from its figure, and the total want of the common voice of the dog, and from general resemblance in other respects, it seems more properly to belong to the wolf than dog kind.

By the time Dr. Caius wrote about English dogs, the Renaissance was

Knight and Hounds Pursue a Woman, by Boticelli (ca. 1482). Courtesy The Prado, Madrid.

Noble Dog. Detail from LAS MENINAS, by Diego Velasquez (ca 1635-1636). Courtesy The Prado, Madrid.

ADORATION OF THE MAGI, by Titian (1477-1576). Note dog using post. The Cleveland Museum of Art. Purchase, Mr. and Mrs. William H. Marlatt Fund.

Big dog with child and dwarf. Painted by Jan Fyt, about 1650. Courtesy Staatliche Kunstsammlungen, Dresden.

in full swing. Artists were painting court scenes as well as Biblical, Greek, and Roman subjects. They included dogs in their paintings of people, often hunting dogs, particularly in the period from 1200 to 1500. But more and more, the dogs pictured were of other breeds, frequently toy dogs. The pictures were of royalty with their loved pets.

Nowhere was this more true than in Sweden. In 1964, John Bernstrom published an immensely valuable little book for the Swedish Kennel Club called *Herre Och Hund*. It consists of fifty-two pictures in black and white, along with explanations, placed in chronological order from 1500 B.C. to A.D. 1749. It is quite possible to recognize most of the dogs pictured by breed—Greyhounds, Mastiffs, northern breeds, Dachshunds, Pugs, dogs similar to modern Papillons, and so on. The book covers the entire Renaissance and is highly recommended as further reading.

LAZARUS AND THE RICH MAN. Italian painting by Jacopo Bassano (1510-1592). Dog may be docked-tailed hunting dog. The Cleveland Museum of Art. Purchase, Delia E. Holden Fund.

THE DEATH OF ADONIS, by Jusepe de Ribera (1591-1652). Note dog
with English Setter type head. The Cleveland Museum of Art. Purchase,
Mr. and Mrs. William H. Marlatt Fund.

TOBIAS AND THE ANGEL. Painting by Giovanni Antonio Guardi
(1698-1760). Dog is probably a hunting dog of Setter type. The Cleveland
Museum of Art. Purchase, Mr. and Mrs. William H. Marlatt Fund.

131

Greenland Eskimo Girl and Dogs, painting by Leon Cogniet. The Cleveland Museum of
Art. Bequest of Noah L. Butkin.

15.   The Arctic—The Eskimos

About four thousand years ago, a mysterious people wandered across Arctic North America. Almost nothing is known about them. They used flaked stone tools, but the little evidence that remains of them indicates they were not Eskimos. One guess is that they were Ice Age hunters who were following the retreating ice and game herds as they moved north. The people disappeared. No one knows why or where they went. One supposition is that they returned to the area of their beginnings or at least deep into Asia.

Between 700 and 600 B.C., another mysterious group arrived in the north. Apparently they came from Asia, crossed the Bering Strait, and settled on the shores of Alaska. One of their sites is called Choris. Here, they lived in oval pit houses, and they made pottery. Their refuse piles, or middens, indicate that they lived on caribou, seals, other sea mammals, and even Arctic fowl.

They also played a fortune-telling game, now called scapulimancy, in which the future is predicted by examining fire-cracked shoulder blades. The Chinese played the game at least forty-five hundred years ago, using the shoulder blades of sheep. The Chukchi and the Tungus of eastern Siberia also played the game and still do. However, the Eskimos do not play it and apparently never did.

The Choris people, too, disappeared, and again no one knows what happened to them. Perhaps, like the earlier Arctic migrants, they also returned to Siberian Asia.

Many students of the Arctic and ethnography believe the Eskimos arrived in North America no earlier than A.D. 500. In their way, the Eskimos are as mysterious as the other two peoples have been. Their language differs from that of any other people, despite many attempts by researchers to find a relationship. They have remarkably small hands and feet, very narrow nose bridges, and their blood type (B) is different from any of their neighbors. Even their ear wax differs from other peoples', and they have shovel-shaped incisors.

The Eskimos spread across the North American Arctic and reached as far as Greenland. Then they retraced their steps to Alaska, leaving some of their members in Greenland and a smaller number in the Canadian Arctic. The smaller Canadian population may be attributable to the richer harvest of fish and sea mammals on both sides of the continent. Another small group remained and still exists on the Asiatic side of the Bering Sea.

It is unknown whether the first migrants had dogs, even whether the Choris people did. Similarly, no one knows when the Eskimos got dogs. Yet it is unthinkable that either the first people or the Eskimos could have migrated across the Arctic without the means of transportation supplied by dogs.

Many students of the Arctic and its peoples have said that the reindeer was used for hauling sledges long before dogs were put to harness. The earliest reference to reindeer is in a Chinese chronicle. In A.D. 499, a Buddhist monk reported seeing reindeer hauling sledges in the lands far north of China. He reported that the people made cream of reindeer milk.

A T'ang Dynasty (618-906) chronicle observed that a far northern tribe had neither sheep nor horses but kept reindeer in the manner of cattle and horses. It said the animals subsisted on moss and were trained to draw sledges. The report continued, noting that reindeer skins were used for making clothing and that reindeer yielded four teacups full of milk in twenty-four hours.

Berthold Laufer is certainly the world's greatest authority on the domestication and use of reindeer. Laufer lived among peoples whose cultures are partially based on dog breeding. These included the Gilyak, Ainu, Olca, and Golde people who lived on Sakhalin Island, the Kuriles, and Hokaido Island. He also lived with reindeer-breeding Tungusians, whom he (along with A. von Middendorff) considered to be the aristocracy of Siberia.

Because the Chukchi and the Eskimos on both sides of the Bering Sea did not know of reindeer and used dog sleds for transportation, Laufer concluded that the use of dogs as draft animals is far older than the use of reindeer. In "Reindeer and its Domestication," published in the 1917 *Memoirs of the American Anthropological Association,* Laufer wrote:

From this wide geographical distribution covering the Old and New Worlds, it necessarily follows that the employment of the dog for the sledge is far older in time than that of the reindeer for the same purpose. Although strictly mathematical proof cannot be put forward, the ethnographical facts well warrant the conclusion that the reindeer-sledge is based on the dog-sledge, and that reindeer driving sprang into existence as a perfectly conscious and volitional imitation of driving with dogs. This being the case, it is clear that the reindeer people must have profited from the experience of the dog-drivers, and reproduced many of their methods.

The Lapps, Ostyaks, Woguls, and Samoyeds used dogs to guard reindeer herds, but the Tungus, Koryak, and Chukchi isolated dogs from theirs. A curious travel book was written by a French Jesuit monk named Phillippe Avril. His *Travels Into Divers Parts of Europe and Asia* was published in an English translation in London in 1693. Avril got only as far as Moscow before being turned back from his travels, so much of what he learned about Asia was by word of mouth. He wrote,

To make the reindeer go more swift, they tie a great dog behind, that scaring the poor beast with his barking, sets her to running with that speed, as to draw her burthen no less than forty leagues in a day.

Laufer observed that since reindeer existed on moss, travelers did not have to carry food for them, as was necessary when using dogs. He added that, in an emergency, a reindeer could be slaughtered for food. Of course, in an emergency, dogs could be used for food, too. And they were. Many an Arctic explorer remarked that if a marooned Eskimo party ran out of food and had to begin eating the dogs, the party was doomed. History often proved the point.

This is one reason it seems likely that even those earliest wanderers across Arctic North America must have had dogs. Dogs had been domesticated long before four thousand years ago. As descendants of the cave artists, the Ice Age hunters could well have formed a bond with dogs. From wherever they originated, the people must have come across the animals, and travel without them must have been nearly impossible.

What were the dogs like? Probably they were early members of the great Northern Forest dogs, linked with the Spitz family. And they probably were not much different from those we know today.

Mastiff or Newfoundland type dog, possibly from Tibet or brought by European traders to China. Seventeenth century. Collection of National Palace Museum, Taiwan, Republic of China.

136

16.   *Tibet*

Greek and Roman writers claimed that the Molossian came from Epirus in the northwest corner of Greece. But they were writing in recent times, compared to the long history of both man and dog. More contemporary authors have suggested that the Molossians were offspring of Tibetan Mastiffs. And I, myself, thought this at one time.

Now I believe the reverse was true, that from the Molossians came the flock guardians—huge, savage dogs, suspicious of all but the shepherd and large enough to keep away wolves and leopards. Singly, they would be no match for either predator; but in pairs, along with the shepherd they alerted, they would make a formidable team. The Mastiffs did not necessarily develop in Tibet, but rather in central Asia. They did not herd flocks, but simply guarded them.

Some authorities have suggested that there were at least three types of Molossian dogs. This may be so, but only the giant type is of interest here. Germany's Max Siber became an expert on the problem of the Tibetan Mastiff in Tibet and Europe and he wrote the book *Der Tibet Hund.* Siber considered these Mastiffs to be almost indistinguishable from the Saint Bernard. He believed the Saint Bernard had its origins in the Mastiff, and he wrote that in Europe he had seen Saint Bernards that could have been Tibetan Mastiffs, and in Tibet, Tibetan Mastiffs that could have been Saint Bernards. Other writers, including Switzerland's Professor H. Kraemer, also believed the Saint Bernard originated in the Tibetan highlands and that it first appeared in Switzerland during Roman times.

In an 1854 work entitled *Physical, Statistical, and Historical,* A. Cunningham wrote, "The only peculiarity that I have noticed about them (the Tibetan Mastiffs) is that the tail is nearly always curled upward on the back, where the hair is displaced by constant rubbing of the tail."

137

This may actually support the belief that the Chow Chow is somehow related to the Tibetan Mastiff and that it is perhaps a descendant of the smaller type of Molossian.

Siber also wrote that in the year 1121 B.C., people in an area west of China sent to the Chinese Emperor Wu Wang a dog of the Tibet race—a Ngao. The dog was four feet high and was trained for man hunting. Because the Chinese foot was shorter than our modern measurements, the dog's height was probably more like thirty to thirty-two inches at the shoulder.

The early Tibetan Mastiffs were rough coated and comparatively short in back. They had heavy muzzles, bodies, and legs, often with double dew-claws on their front legs. Their foreheads were wrinkled, and they were black or brown in color, with white on their chests.

All early writers attested to their savagery, as have modern visitors to Tibet. Thomas Manning, an Englishman who lived several years in China, journeyed into Tibet in September 1811. Unaccredited by either the China or India governments, he seems to have managed the trip because he was able to practice some medicine. Sir Clements Markham published Manning's diary in 1879.* In it, he writes of his disdain for the city of Lhasa.

There is nothing striking, nothing pleasing in its appearance. The habitations are begrimed with dirt and smut. The avenues are full of dogs, some growling and gnawing bits of hide which lie about in profusion and emit a charnel house smell; others limping and looking livid; others ulcerated; others starving and dying, and pecked at by ravens; some dead and preyed upon.

An Indian surveyor named Nain Sing worked in Tibet in 1865 and 1866. He visited one chief (probably a lama) who had a gigantic black Lhasa tied to the door of his tent. "These Tibetan Mastiffs are unpleasantly savage," wrote Sing. Incidentally, the chief seemed to spend most of his time drinking tea and whiskey.

Nain Sing was also instrumental in breaking through a long-standing Tibetan myth. Some areas of the country were once rich with gold fields, and the famed Greek, Herodotus, had reported that huge Tibetan ants dug the gold. The story existed until Sing and Ugyen, another surveyor, visited the region.

*Narrative of the Mission of George Bogle to Tibet and Journey of Thomas Manning to Lhasa (second edition).

138

The gold fields, now exhausted, were located in high mountains. The weather was intensely cold and was made worse by strong winds. Nomads, not ants, mined the gold, and they mined only in winter. To avoid part of the cold, they placed their tents in trenches about ten feet deep. They slept on their hands and knees, piling robes upon their backs. And they worked the gold fields on their hands and knees with clothes packed over their backs. So they probably did look like huge ants.

According to Sing and Ugyen, the nomads were guarded by huge, savage dogs.* At one point, Ugyen was met with hospitality from the people and a boisterous reception by the dogs. He later came upon a guard house at a river bridge, and on either side of the door was chained a fierce Tibetan Mastiff. He described the Tibetan Mastiff as being as large as the English Mastiff, rough-coated, shaggy, and untamably fierce.

Sing and Ugyen also tell of the difficulties experienced by a lama who tried to enter the city.

A solitary wayfarer on foot runs no little risk from the number of savage dogs which prowl around the city walls feeding on offal and human corpses. He had to supply himself with bones and delicacies such as dogs love in order to win his way.

This passage corresponds with earlier discussions of ancient times and the various cultures in which human bodies were thrown to the dogs. The custom has existed in Tibet as far back as written history begins, and it still exists today. In *Tibet the Mysterious*, author T. Hungerford Holdich quotes the following passage by Ugyen.

There are two burial places in Lhasa. The larger of the two is to the northeast of the town called Raga, and the other is near a temple within the walls of Lhasa. Dead bodies are laid on a large flat stone on which places for the limbs have been roughly hollowed out, with their faces to the sky and their limbs stretched out. A smoke is then sent to the sky, and two vultures appear. If these vultures in their flight wheel to the right, then the soul is happy in heaven, otherwise the vultures either turn to the left or disappear. The body is finally torn to pieces and devoured by these birds.

*Report of Chandra Das to the Indian Survey as told to him by Ugyen.

This is the only ceremony alluded to by Ugyen, but it was not the only method for disposing of the dead. Bodies were also cut to pieces by the *Ragyabas,* or scavengers who formed a sort of guild in Lhasa into which was received any outcast or criminal who could not be disposed of otherwise. The Ragyabas then distributed the pieces of corpse among the city dogs. Holdich provides the following:

The Ragyabas are a specially offensive class of the lowest type of Tibetan humanity, who enjoy privileges of their own, one of which appears to be insulting all whom they meet who do not respond to their demand for alms. They are not allowed to build houses or to live otherwise than in huts constituted of mud and the horns of animals .... All writers refer to them and to the mangy savage dogs which feed on the dismembered corpses of defunct Tibetans.

In 1981, Charlotte Salisbury published a book about her travels with her husband Harrison along the "old silk route" through China and Tibet. In *Tibetan Diary, and Travels Along the Old Silk Route,* she, too, writes of the people's methods for disposing of dead bodies. Her account is similar to the one above, but she adds a horrifying sequel. Visiting someone's home, she saw a series of color slides. One showed a dapper gentleman sitting with friends under an awning. Her host remarked that the man was his friend. The next few slides showed the man being skinned, cut up, and fed to waiting vultures, which seemed to be trained to sit patiently for their food.

In her book, Mrs. Salisbury reported that she never saw dogs in China, although she heard them at one place. She found Tibet was a "violent contrast," where dogs were everywhere and slept in the streets and alleys all day long. She also recognized some Lhasa Apsos.

Tibet is believed to have developed several small dog breeds from the Tibetan Mastiff—the Lhasa Apso, Tibetan Terrier, and Tibetan Spaniel. The Lhasa Apso seems to be the current favorite in most countries. But a quarter of a century ago, the prediction was that the Tibetan Terrier would become the most popular and that the other two might disappear.

According to Barry Clifford, writing in Brian Vesey-Fitzgerald's *The Book of the Dog* (published in America in 1946, but earlier in England), the first Tibetan dogs were introduced to Great Britain about 1930. Clifford believed that the Lhasa Apso was "too untidy" to become popular in England and America, and a picture shown in the book would seem to bear him out: The dogs are shown in long, straight coats reaching to the ground.

Clifford was wrong, and the breed has achieved immense popularity world-wide. In America, the first Lhasa to arrive came from the Dalai Lama himself. Today, all three breeds—Lhasa Apso, Tibetan Terrier, and Tibetan Spaniel—are recognized in the United States and Canada.

The Tibetan Terrier is not a true terrier, and the Tibetan Spaniel is not a true spaniel. Whether the Lhasa Apso and Tibetan Terrier are bred down from the Tibetan Mastiff is open to question. Since Tibet had foreign trade in all directions, it seems probable that breeds smaller than the Mastiff were used as well. This would help to account for differences in temperament in the smaller dogs.

The Tibetan Spaniel, however, shows unmistakable evidence of relationship to the short-nosed breeds, such as the Pekingese, Pug, and Japanese Chin. Additional help in dwarfing the dogs might well have come from Greece and Rome. In any case, all three breeds are now so well known in most countries that they need no further comment here.

To make a further statement upon the puzzle of the origin of the Saint Bernard, the similarity between that breed and the Tibetan Mastiff, particularly fifty to one hundred years ago, cannot be ignored. Nor can the appearance of the huge Saint Bernard in the glacial areas of the Alps—a climate roughly similar to that of Tibet—be ignored. Instead, these are unmistakable evidences of the movement of men and animals across vast distances.

Example of early Pekingese Dog. Courtesy National Museum, Taiwan.

141

Fo Dog, or Ch'I Lin, Ch'ing Dynasty (1644-1911), China. The Cleveland Museum of Art. Gift of Mrs. Worcester R. Warner for the Worcester R. Warner Collection.

17.   *China*

Until 1983, few archaeological expeditions had been conducted in China. Consequently, zoological information on its prehistoric animals is still fragmentary. Qu Guo Qin of the Institute of Vertebrate Paleontology and Paleoanthropology, Academia Sinica at Beijing, wrote to me of what little is known.

Early dog materials have been found in at least the following three sites: The Ho Mu-du site (Yu Yao County, Zhejiang Province) has been carbon dated as having existed approximately 6100 B.P. (Before Present). The Xia Wang-gang site (Xi Chuan County, Honan Province) has an estimated date of 6000 B.P. And the Ban-Po site (Xian City, Shenxi Province) has been carbon dated at 6960 B.P., plus or minus one hundred years. These sites of Neolithic settlement are located along the great river valleys where vegetation was lush. Two domestic animals were found in their remains—the domestic dog and the pig. At first, this seems puzzling. Since sheep and goats were domesticated long before the pig, why were they not also found?

Qu Guo Qin and Stanley J. Olsen, who is a University of Arizona professor and a world-renowned authority on dog fossils, have an excellent explanation for this. Lush vegetation proved unsuitable for sheep, but it was ideal for swine and swine culture. Even today, mutton does not normally appear in Chinese diets.

The Chinese Book of Rites classified dogs in three ways—as house pets or guardians; as hunting dogs, which were further classified; and as food. Chinese children were taught from a standard text, which reported that a sixth of China's meat came from dogs and horses. Cats, too, were eaten.

An English writer, commenting upon a pair of Chow Chows sent to England in 1802, wrote that they were:

143

English Greyhound type imported to China, ninteenth century. Collection of National Palace Museum, Taiwan, Republic of China.

"Painted by the imperial brush of Tzu Hsi, Empress Dowager, in the ninth year of T'ung Chih (1870) in the last ten days of the third month of Spring"

144

Greyhound on Han bas-relief of Wu Liang. Harris after Chavennes: La Sculpture en Pierre en Chine.

Hunting dogs on Han Period bas-relief. Note beaters and hawk. Harris after Kin Shih So.

Ceramic dog of Chow Chow type from Han Period. After Laufer in Chinese pottery of the Han Dynasty.

... such as are fattened in that country for the purpose of being eaten; they are about the size of a moderate spaniel; of a pale yellow color, with coarse bristling hairs on their backs; sharp upright ears and peaked heads; which gives them a very fox-like appearance. Their hind legs are unusually straight without any bend at the back or ham, to such a degree as to give them an awkward gait when they trot. When they are in motion, their tails are curved high over their backs like those of some hounds, and have a bare space . . . . Their eyes are jet black, small and piercing; the insides of their lips and mouth of the same color, and their tongue blue. (*White's Natural History of Selborne*, 1882, Vol. II, p. 77.)

The classification of dogs as food is even more interesting considering that, as early as 2852 B.C., the Chinese seem to have believed that a dog of many colors created the world. (North American Indians gave this honor to the coyote.) Dogs also were believed to be effective in warding off evil, and so they were buried under the city gates. During the Chou Dynasty (1028-221 B.C.), dogs began to be buried with their masters.

Now dogs have accompanied their masters wherever they have wandered in all sections of the globe. And even in prehistoric times, there seems to have been two major trade routes into and out of China. One, the great silk route, led from what is now Beijing (Peking) to Xpan, and then on to Chengdu, Lhasa in Tibet, Shigatse, Katmandu, and south into India. The second went from Xpan to Lanzhou, Dunhuang, Turpan, Urumqi, and on into inner Asia. And dogs—fancy toy dogs, hunting dogs, and fighting dogs—were valuable trade articles on these routes.

In today's industrialized civilization it can be hard to understand the passion that ancient people—even those of one hundred and fifty years ago—had for hunting, hunting dogs, and toy dogs. But dogs of all sorts were bartered back and forth. Traders carried Maltese dogs to the Orient, and dogs of Pekingese type went to all of Europe, including the British Isles. The trade was greatly increased when the sea routes were opened by intrepid navigators.

The British, great animal breeders then as now, very early developed superior strains of the coursing breeds, the English Greyhound being one. The Scots developed the Scottish Deerhound, and the Irish, the Irish Wolfhound. These were superior to the Greyhounds of China, as well as to the Wolfhounds of the Mongols. Imports from the British Isles improved the Asiatic dogs, and various strains developed—particularly in Greyhounds—with the Chinese having both smooth and long-haired Greyhounds and the Mongols having long-haired Wolfhounds. Eventually the superiority of the British dogs caused the disappearance of the native breeds. But another factor in their disappearance was the end of the nobility's massive hunting parties.

The Chinese Emperor would train his armies in the hunting fields. Thousands of men and as many dogs would form a line. The soldiers then became either huntsmen or beaters, and no game could escape. The sight of such an army must have impressed the nomads and traders who came from the China borders. Indeed, Marco Polo wrote of two Chinese barons, each of whom maintained ten thousand men, all dressed alike, except that those of one baron wore red and those of the other wore blue. The barons also had charge of the dogs, "fleet and slow, and of the mastiffs." When the Great Khan or a prince went hunting, the twenty thousand men, with about five thousand dogs, would amass as follows: One baron and his men and dogs would split right, the other would go left, and the whole line would extend for a full day's journey.

True Chinese civilization began about five thousand years ago. Writing was developed about 1650 B.C., roughly the same time that city life began. Texts make only occasional references to dogs, but as the centuries passed, the Chinese became passionate dog breeders. For one thing, dogs were considered treasures, and all treasures belonged to the Emperor. So, if people could breed a dog pleasing to the Emperor, good fortune, high position, and money would be theirs.

Some of the dogs bred were small enough to be carried by soldiers, either in front of the saddle or behind. From rare illustrations, these appear to have been of Greyhound type. The Chinese also were passionate gamblers, and dog races seem to have been held, with Greyhound-like dogs being favored.

Many of the Chinese dogs were so small they could lie under the table—and Chinese tables were very short-legged. For then, as now, people sat on pillows on the floor when they ate, a custom also observed by many Japanese. From such small dogs came the Pekingese, the Pug, and, in Japan, the Chin. But evidence suggests that, as with the coursing dogs, the modern dogs of these small breeds owe their present conformation to imports from Europe, particularly Great Britain. And so great was the Dutch passion for the Pug that it has been called the Dutch Pug.

The cult that demanded a lap dog that looked like a diminutive of the

Chinese conception of a lion reached a peak between 1820 and 1860. The breed was sponsored by the Empress Tzu Hsi. In her time, the breeding of dogs was taken over as an imperial function with a large number of eunuchs in charge. When the British sacked Peking in 1860, the Empress gave orders that all the sacred dogs should be destroyed so as not to fall into the hands of the "white devils." But some were discovered, confiscated, and sent to England, beginning the modern cult of the Pekingese.

The Shih Tzu (properly pronounced "sheed zu") is the result of crossing Lhasa Apsos with Pekingese. Once the breed had become standardized, the Kennel Club of England recognized it. The Shih Tzu then spread to the United States. But for some years The American Kennel Club refused to recognize the breed because of its known crossmating with Pekingese. It is considered a Chinese breed.

Charlotte Salisbury reported in her book that she never saw any dogs in China, although she heard a few barking in Dunhuang. The reason would appear to be orders by Mao Tse Tung and other Communist officials. They believed dogs and cats consumed too much food that could be used by people. So they ordered the animals' extinction. Similar orders were reissued in late 1983.

In March 1959, I judged a dog show in Hong Kong. Neither at that show, nor at one in 1962, were there any Chow Chows. I was told by Chinese people that there were no Chows left in China, except for one owned by the Dutch ambassador. That dog had a broken leg and could not be shown. Further, it was Belgian bred.

One Shar Pei was shown at the 1959 show. It was quite savage and had to be held by two people. Even then, I had to judge it from a distance because it continually tried to attack me. I was told it was the last living Shar Pei in China. However, hundreds have been rounded up and sold to Americans in the years since then. (The owner of the above dog has denied it tried to attack me.)

Chinese Coursing Dogs being carried on horseback. Collection of the National Palace Museum, Taiwan, Republic of China.

Kara Shishi (literally China Lion). Sculpture, Mamakura Period (1200 to 1400 A.D.), Japan. The Cleveland Museum of Art. Purchase, Dudley P. Allen Fund.

18.   *Japan*

To trace the history of dogs in any culture, one must trace the history of man himself. In such a study, some remarkable surprises are encountered. And this is the case with Japan.

No one knows who the original people of Japan were. Most have heard of the Ainu, often called the "hairy Ainu" because they had such luxuriant body hair, almost like pelts in some males. And both sexes had a passion for this hair. Of course, it helped to keep them warm, which was no inconsiderable bonus in the climate of the Japanese northern islands. At one time, Ainu women even tattooed mustaches on their upper lips.

Anthropologists wonder about the origin of the Ainu people. Based on the theory of the cultural center, one assumes they migrated from somewhere, but it also is possible that they always inhabited the islands. Certainly, at one time, they occupied the entire archipelago.

Aside from the profusion of body hair, the Ainu differ from their nothern Asiatic neighbors in many other respects. They do not have shovel-shaped incisors. Their ear wax is sticky, not crumbly. Their finger ridges have more whorls than loops. Their eye sockets are not almond shaped, and the lids are not double-folded. Finally, their language defies exact analysis.

People have always wondered whether the "cave men" were as hairy as artists have tended to picture them. It is tempting to think that those Ainu who have remained pure blooded are the last survivors from the old Stone Age or even earlier. Some anatomists have suggested that Ainu skulls seem faintly Neanderthaloid.

Perhaps as early as 8500 B.C., a new people, or at least a new culture, began to develop in Japan. It is called the Jomon Culture, and its people are called the Jomons. They may have migrated to the islands, or they may have been the descendants of the Ainu. In the latter case, as an intense and fast-advancing culture began to develop, the more primitive Ainu tribes were forced farther and farther to the north.

151

Puppies of Akita type. Edo Period, about 1770. Courtesy National Museum, Tokyo, Japan.

Old woman with puppies. Edo Period, about 1780. Courtesy National Museum, Tokyo, Japan.

Jomon skulls are very similar to those of the Ainu. Anthropologist Dr. Julius Lips once told me that the Cro-Magnons had not annihilated the Neanderthals, but had simply bred them out of existence. "Look carefully," he said, "you'll spot people with Neanderthal characteristics, however faint they may be." So the Ainu-Jomon relationship is not impossible.

Jomon actually means "cord-marked," and the Jomons may have been the world's first pottery makers. The Jomons and the Ainu placed small clay figures of females in their graves. Both seem to have worshipped the female principle, and the clay figurines represent goddesses.

The Jomons were making cord-marked pottery by 7500 B.C.; gradually that pottery began to show highly skilled and very sensitive workmanship. A major surprise is that a cord-marked bowl of obvious Jomon quality was found in a shell heap on the coast of Ecuador. It is carbon dated at 3000 B.C., which is several millenia before Ecuadorian Indians could show any skill at pottery making. One can only guess that Jomon fishermen or explorers were blown across the South Pacific.

Although the Jomons were hunters and fishermen, primarily the latter, they also had tools of a type used for agriculture. And they had domesticated dogs, which seem to have been used for hunting deer, wild boar, and bear.

Science reports from The Yokohama National University list canid skeletal remains found in the Akiyoshi-dai Cave in Yamaguchi Prefecture. They date from the Upper Pleistocene. Somewhat like the case with the Star Carr canid bones in England, scientists are not yet sure whether the bones are those of a domesticated dog.

But in the Natsushima Shell Mounds, Kanagawa Prefecture, skeletal remains of what are undeniably domesticated dogs were found. They have been carbon dated at 9300 B.P. Dog remains also were found at Kamiluro-iwa, Ehine Prefecture, and they date from 8500 to 8000 B.P.

It is interesting that the Kanagawa Prefecture dog bones were found in a shell mound, which is a heap of shells left by ancient fishermen after extracting the meat. As noted before, the Jomons were primarily fishermen. And the Ainu used, and still use, dogs for fishing. They have trained their dogs to swim out to sea, to form three sides of a square, and by raising a commotion, to drive fish close to shore. Thus, they form a sort of living trawl, with an occasional dog being able to catch a fish. They also have been taught to catch fish in rivers.

At some time during the long past, the Japanese Archipelago was a part of Asia, just as Britain was a part of Europe and the Bering Strait a land bridge between Asia and North America. The separation permitted the island people to develop their own distinctive culture. And this was true also of the dogs.

A new people arrived in the islands about 300 B.C. Called the Yayoi, their origins are about as obscure as are those of the Ainu and the Jomons. It is believed they came from Korea, and, indeed, the Japanese claimed sovereignty over Korea for a long time.

At any rate, the Yayoi consolidated Japan into a nation. And it is from that period that we begin to get some real ideas of what the native dogs were like. They fell within the northern types of Asia. They had rather heavy heads; broad, deep muzzles; prick ears; a rather heavy body, not strongly angulated at the stifle joint; and curled tails. They were bred for hunting but also served as home and property guardians.

By the early part of the fifth century, times were prosperous, and trade among Japan, China, and Korea flourished. Chinese emperors, such as Ch'ih T'ung (690-696) and Tien Wu Ti (673-686), sent presents of small pet dogs to Japan. These were enthusiastically received by such Japanese emperors as Tenmu (673-686).

The dog known as the Japanese Chin most likely developed at this time, although much later there probably was an infusion of English Toy Spaniel blood. It is worth noting that *Chin* seems to be a combination of two root words meaning *China Dog*.

Among other dogs sent to Japan was a breed called the Wo Tzu or Chinese Pai dog. As early as the first century, the Chinese describe this dog as an "under the table breed." It was short-legged and "short-headed." Since the Chinese table was set low and people sat on pillows to eat from it, the dog obviously had to be very small.

The Portuguese captured Goa in 1510 and established trade relations with Japan in 1549. The Dutch and English were not far behind. They wooed the Japanese with expensive gifts, made war among themselves, and were banished from Japan, or to European trade shelters, such as Macao or India. But if the Europeans brought dogs as presents to Japan, the Japanese almost certainly sent similar presents to Europe.

A Captain Saris, who visited the court of the Daimio of Hirado in 1614, wrote home to England to his commanding general recommending that among presents to be sent should be "a mastife, a watter spaniell, and a fine Greyhound."* These were to be presents to the Daimio's son. Richard Cooke, chief factor for Japan of the East India Company from

Wood sculpture of a dog. About 2500 B.P. Courtesy Kozanji Temple Museum, Tokyo, Japan.

1615 to 1623, mentions receiving a present from the Japanese of a "great black dogg" in exchange for some goldfish, which then were a rarity in Japan.**

Japan was opened to the West again during the great Meiji Era (1867-1912) and a heavy influx of foreign visitors occurred. Many brought dogs that became so popular the local breeds were brought nearly to the point of extinction. The local breeds were then lumped together as the Ji Inu. Those remaining in the mountains, where they were still used for hunting, were called the Kas Kari Inu, which means hunting dogs. Beginning in the Taisho Period (1912-1926) and in the present Showa Period, the Hihon Ken Hozon Kai (Dogs of Japan Preservation Club) rescued the local breeds from extinction and brought them to their present state of excellence.

Today, the Japanese divide their native dogs into four size groups. The smallest is a Japanese Chin which is sometimes called a Japanese Spaniel, even by the Japanese. Among the dogs of the northern type, the Shiba Inu is the smallest. Then come the middle sized dogs—the Hokkaido Ken, Akita Matagi Inu, Kai Ken, Kisnu Ken, and the Akita Ken, which is the largest. The massive and mighty Tosa Ken is the largest of Japanese dogs. In earlier times, it was used as a fighting dog. Obviously of Mastiff origin, it would appear to be closer to an original Mastiff type than is the Chinese Shar Pei. However, almost nothing can be determined about its origins.

The Japanese have long had a passion for diminutive things. Bonzai trees and the Japanese Chin are examples of this. That the Chin is related to the Pekingese and the Pug cannot be doubted, but as said earlier, it unquestionably contains English Toy Spaniel blood as well.

---

*Quoted by Ash based on East India Company records.
**East India Company records quoted by V.W.F. Collier in *Dogs of China and Japan* (Stokes, 1921, London).

An Assembly of Dervishes, Mughal School, 1650 A.D. Prince of Wales Museum of Western India, Bombay.

19.   *India, Afghanistan, Arabia*

The East, meaning in this case, Arabia, Afghanistan, and India, was the home of a group of dogs known as Tazi Kutha, or the running dog. The Greeks and Romans had called their running dogs gaze hounds. The British had called their coursing dogs Greyhounds. And in recent times, the dogs of the East have been called Eastern Greyhounds.

H. W. Bush was a Christian minister and missionary who spent many years in India, and who travelled extensively in Arabia and Afghanistan. He had a passionate interest in running hounds, and he remains one of the greatest authorities on them. His fluent knowledge of the Indian language and Arabic helped him greatly.

J. Sidney Turner, "chairman of the committee" of the Kennel Club in London, published *The Kennel Encyclopaedia* in 1907. Since Reverend Bush was the greatest authority on the Eastern Greyhounds, Turner selected Bush to write a chapter on them.

Bush began with the Saluki, which he believed was the parent of all the other breeds. He consulted a moulvie, or learned doctor of Islamic law, concerning the name of the breed. The moulvie told him that the name came from the birthplace of the breed, a town called Saluquia in Yemen. The Arabic doctor then wrote,

> The most famous is the Persian Saluqui or Saluqi of Bakkan, and is the biggest kind of them and most tearing one of its chase. It has very long smooth hair and the colour of the former (Persian) is deep yellow, and of the latter yellowish and white. The Arabian Saluqi is large in size and very strong, and his colour varies according to the variety of his birth and origin, and is kept by most of the Bedouins, and they chase deers and hares by means of it.

159

Shahu Maharaj. Decconi School. Copy made at Satara in 1854. Prince of Wales Museum of Western India, Bombay.

Portrait of a hunting hound (1803 period), School of Rajasthani Deogarh. Prince of Wales Museum of Western India, Bombay.

161

It seems unlikely that the Saluki originated in Yemen. The country is mountainous, with an average elevation of nine thousand feet and a maximum of more than twelve thousand. It is obvious that Bush himself did not believe the moulvie, for he states that the Saluki originated in Egypt. He was, of course, familiar with the Egyptian tomb paintings of Saluki-like dogs. But it must be remembered that in terms of time, Egypt is only minutes away from us. Bush also states his belief that dogs came down from the mountains and tended to lose their long coats.

The great variety and yet similarity of the Eastern Greyhounds, plus ancient paintings, make it virtually certain that the entire race had its origins in the vast subcontinent of India, or on the road from the mountains of Tibet, down the Indus valley, and other roads leading into India. Bush does state in his conclusion that the Arab and Persian hounds are identical, "differing only in size and coat, while the Afghan is descended from the Seistan section of the Persian hound."

With his article, Bush had pictures of two Salukis. Both come from the island of Bahrain. Bahrain was an ancient island trading post between India and Arabia. (As an aside, I have received a letter from the Bahrain Kennel Club asking for information on the origin of the Saluki.)

An alternate claim has been made for the origin of the Saluki name. It was said to derive from the Grecian town of Seleucia. Reverend Bush roundly condemned this and blamed the "canine press" for using such terms as Slughi, Sleughi, and Sloughi. He pointed out that the word slughi means "the young of a cow which has cast off six of its front teeth, and has thus become a grown animal." Today, however, a separate but very similar breed in North Africa is called officially the Sleughi.

In his list of Eastern Greyhounds, Bush includes Mahrattas, Rampurs, Banjaras, Poligars, and Persian and Arab hounds, and Afghans. Bush describes an Afghan perfectly. And what he says about Afghan temperament in those days is worth repeating.

They are nasty, savage beasts, especially in the neighborhood of their own village, and bite white and black men indiscriminately, though they have a preference for sampling the white. When obtained as pups they can be trained and become amenable to English rule, but they all possess an inborn tendency to wander off on the scavenge when left loose.

Bush included with his article a picture of Zardin, a dog which was taken to England, and was at first called a Persian Greyhound. But today he is considered to have been an Afghan. A modern Afghan book laments that Zardin did not have any offspring. But he did, and Bush also included a picture of a puppy sired by Zardin. The pup is obviously of Afghan type.

The Borzoi once was called the Russian Wolfhound. One suggestion is that the breed was developed by crossing a Steppe Greyhound with a Collie, or with a dog of Collie type and coat. Bush comes to no conclusion as to the dog's origin, but does write, "The Siberian Wolfhound and its near relation, the Borzoi, may even come from the same original stock."

In closing this chapter we mention the now extinct Rampur Hound. It originated in Central India and, as were so many of the Eastern Greyhounds, was quite savage. But it had amazing endurance, although it was slower than the English Greyhound. Sportsmen crossed the two to give the English dog greater stamina and stronger feet. Strangely, the Rampur was virtually hairless, and an occasional one was said to have a topknot such as the Chinese Crested has.

A Procession, Mughal School. Second decade of seventeenth century. Prince of Wales Museum of Western India, Bombay.

163

Conquistadores' dogs escaped in large numbers and were seized by the Indians. Two types developed: one with drop ears, the other with erect ears. Here a native family prepares for a fete. Courtesy of Professor Procopio Del Valle.

Spanish Conquistadores and their dogs attack the Indians in this early Spanish painting. Courtesy of Professor Procopio Del Valle.

164

20.   North and South America

The traditional view of the origin of the Indians of North and South America is that they came from Asia. It is theorized that they crossed the Bering Strait during a cold interval of the Ice Age when the sea level had dropped until dry land was exposed. The migrants, being wanderers and explorers, may have continued to go south, or successive waves of other migrants may have driven them farther and farther south until they reached Patagonia and Tierra del Fuego at the tip of South America.

I remember reading somewhere that the remains of a charcoal fire had been found in southern Chile in a mountain cave and had been carbon dated at 29,000 B.C. I cannot now find the report. But if it is true, it places man in the New World far earlier than anyone had supposed. However, I cannot vouch for the authenticity of this.

A very daring theory has been advanced that the wide diversity in human types is the result of independent development from similar but not identical stock. Thus, according to this theory, the South American Indians are not related to those of North America.

Today, these theories are being challenged by new discoveries, discoveries that indicate explorers and traders covered much of North America and large areas of South America even before the time of Christ. Indeed, Thomas Jefferson believed there was some sort of connection between the Indians of North America and the people of North Africa. But most of the evidence he gathered was destroyed when a vandal stole his trunk. Since Jefferson's time, hundreds of strange rock inscriptions have been discovered across the length and breadth of America. Learning who made them and what they mean has been the focus of considerable research by Dr. Barry Fell, an emeritus professor at

Harvard University. Dr. Fell also is president of the Epigraphic Society, members of which are experts at deciphering ancient inscriptions. Some, including Dr. Fell, have been able to break military codes and did so in World War II.

Fell has published eight books containing decipherments of ancient inscriptions. He and others have collected large numbers of pre-Christian coins. They have photographed hundreds of rock inscriptions and have made replicas of them. In deciphering these, Fell has followed Jefferson's suspicion and gone to North Africa, where authorities on ancient languages have verified his work.

His 1977 book, *America, B.C.,* startled American historians and archaeologists, leaving them skeptical and indignant. But then Fell published a second book in 1980. *Saga America* is loaded with hundreds of examples, drawings, coins, and so on, with messages in various North African languages of pre-Christian times. There now can be no doubt that this hemisphere was visited from both the Atlantic and the Pacific, and that extensive explorations were undertaken by the visitors.

These explorations took place in South America as well. The late Padre Carlo Crespi of Santa Maria Auxillodora Parish, at Cuenca, Ecuador, made a careful collection of pre-Columbian artifacts found by peasants. Phoenicians on the island of Cyprus were well known for making miniature reproductions of Assyrian and Babylonian stone carvings. Two such reproductions, probably made between 600 and 800 B.C., are in this collection.

Additionally, as pointed out earlier, a Jomon vase has been found in a shell heap in Ecuador. It is carbon dated at 3000 B.C., long before the art of pottery making was known to South America. Based on this discovery, it appears that Jomon seamen visited Ecuador. Perhaps they had been blown far off their course, but it is more likely that they were explorers, driven to discover what was on the other side of the great ocean.

It seems unlikely that these early wanderers, explorers, traders, and fishermen were accompanied by their dogs. Of course, those who followed the explorations of Eric the Red and his son, Leif the Lucky, would have brought along theirs, because they came to colonize. But they did not stay. Their colonies perished, and presumably any survivors and their dogs returned to Iceland or to Europe. And if Carthaginian, Phoenician, Libyan, or other traders carried dogs, they probably did not bring a sufficient number for the animals to become established in the New World. At any rate, as will be seen later, they left no lasting impression. For distinct races of dogs did not develop in the Americas at those early times.

If this is puzzling, it is less so than a series of puzzles regarding the development of the dog. It is generally agreed that the ancestors of both the horse and the dog developed in North America. One can visit the American Museum of Natural History in New York and see the skeletons, including that of Eohippus, a four-toed horse about the size of a fox. The skeletons grow larger until they reach the size of the modern horse. (Eohippus has been classified by some with the European Hycotherium.)

The dog's early ancestors, those reponsible for the entire canid family, also existed in North America. Then the ancestors of both horse and dog disappeared. Their future development was elsewhere, for the most part, in Asia. No one knows why this happened.

Horses did not return to America until the Spaniards brought them in the early 1500s. Then they spread like wildfire all across the American West. They bred in the wild in huge numbers, proving that the environment was perfect for them. Generations of living in the wild did not, however, make them wild animals. They were easily returned to full domesticity.

What happened to the dog is the next puzzle. There are two theories, and they do not agree. One is based on the fossil record; the other is the testimony of the first educated people who came to the Americas.

The great anthropologist, Dr. Barbara Lawrence, found the fossil bones of a dog in the Jaguar Cave, Birch Creek Valley, Lemhi County, Idaho. The bones have been carbon dated at 9500 to 8400 B.C. The animal thus lived as many as eleven thousand years ago. And it had shared the cave with man. Based on Fell's work, which indicates that ancient explorers, wanderers, and traders visited the western world long before the Christian era, it is tempting to speculate that the Jaguar Cave dog was not a native of North America. Perhaps it accompanied explorers who crossed either of the great oceans by ship, or who travelled by foot across the Bering Strait.

As mentioned before, Stanley J. Olsen is possibly the world's greatest authority on fossil dogs in North America. In 1970, in the *Bulletin of the Georgia Academy of Science*, he wrote of "Two Pre-Columbian Dog Burials From Georgia." He begins by writing:

Burials of domesticated dogs (*Canis familiaris*) of pre-Columbian Age,

167

are not commonly encountered anywhere in the United States. However, they are better known from sites in the southwest (Allen, 1920; Lawrence, 1944; Olsen, 1968) although Indian dogs from the Southeast have been referred to and compared.

Dr. Olsen was writing about dog burials estimated to have taken place about 500 B.C. These dogs, which were buried eleven miles from Augusta, Georgia, appear to have been carefully buried, as if they had been loyal and devoted comrades of men—men who had journeyed a long way from home. Since 500 B.C. is the time when explorers and traders from North Africa presumably were visiting America, it is tempting to speculate that the dogs came from North Africa.

So far as I have been able to discover, 500 B.C. is about the earliest date for the domesticated dog in America, except for the Jaguar Cave dog. This is a very long span of time, a wide gap in our knowledge of the history of the dog.

I believe that Stanley Olsen and Barbara Lawrence stand at the top of the list of American anthropologists and paleoarchaeologists—archeologists who study fossils—who have produced all that we know of the pre-Columbian dogs of North America. But there is a different and sharply opposite view of the dogs of North and South America. One cannot doubt the testimony of the fossil record, but neither can one doubt the reports of the first educated men to come to America.

In one sense, Columbus was a magnificent failure. He had promised the Spanish monarchs that he would discover a new route to the Orient, and he promised them spices and gold. He found no gold, nor did he find the kinds of spices Europe expected. It is doubtful that he ever touched the continent of North America, but great raids upon the New World followed him.

In North America, Cortez began the conquest of Mexico in 1519, but collided with the great Aztec empire. Pizarro sailed for Peru in 1531, and upon his arrival faced the even greater empire of the Incas. The Aztecs had been quite recent invaders of the Valley of Mexico. They had subjugated the neighboring tribes with great cruelty and had made many enemies. The Incas, too, had only a few generations of sovereignty over their empire.

Two men, both great historians, had dedicated their lives to Mexico. Manuel Orozco y Berra was a Mexican scholar. His *Historia Antigua y de la Conquista de Mexico* was published in 1880. The second was the

168

American historian, William H. Prescott. The nearly blind historian, who could use his one eye only for an hour a day, published his *Conquest of Mexico* in 1843, and his *Conquest of Peru* in 1847.

Rather ruefully, it seems to me, Prescott says the following in his *Conquest of Mexico:*

> The resemblance of the different species of those in the Old World, with which no one of them, however, was identical, led to a perpetual confusion in the nomenclature of the Spaniards, as it has since done in that of better instructed naturalists.

Prescott also wrote that the Aztecs had no useful domestic animals. Even so, some of his "better instructed naturalists" tended to place the Alco in Mexico. But Alco is an Incan word, and these two high-level cultures—Aztec in Mexico and Inca in Peru—knew nothing of each other.

A more contemporary example of the "perpetual confusion in the nomenclature" may be in Dr. Glover M. Allen's use of the word Techichi.

Dr. Allen, of Harvard University, published a famous monograph titled "Dogs of the American Aborigines" in 1920. He believed he could identify seventeen breeds of dogs, most of which came from the Southwest. However, he felt that these breeds could be reduced to two basic groups—large dogs and small. Allen called one group, the Techichi. In this, I think he was making a serious mistake.

Manuel Orozco y Berra, the famed Mexican historian who devoted his life to studying the years before and after the Spanish conquest, mentions the Techichi. He says the Spaniards called it a dog because it resembled one. He says it had a melancholy aspect and was mute. The Spaniards ate the Techichi, and because they ate all of them, there is no real information as to what it was. Chichi was an Aztec root word for mammal.

Explorers and conquistadors, starting with Columbus, mentioned a strange native dog. It moved in packs and was described as being horribly deformed and mute. It could climb trees. It also was delicious to eat. Richard Eden, in his *Decades of the Newe Worlde or West India,* wrote in the early 1500s about the Caribbean Islands.

. . . yet founde they there four dogges of marvelous deformed shape,

Cruel Portuguese forces Indian to tow him across the river. The dog with a heavily spiked collar follows. Courtesy Professor Procopio Del Valle.

Native family, in a sylvan jungle setting, roasts a giant frog. Courtesy Professor Procopio Del Valle.

Modern descendant of the savage dogs which the
Portuguese used in subjugating the Indians of Brazil.
He is the Fila Brazileiro Ch. E'Bana Do Sobrado,
owned by Rafael Martim of Belo Horizonte. Courtesy
Professor Procopio Del Valle.

and such as coulde not barke. This kynd of dogges, they eate as we do goates.

In fact, the Spaniards did eat all they could find, as well as every other animal the Aztecs had domesticated. The reason was a perpetual shortage of meat.

The great naturalist Norman J. Berrill wrote a book called *Journey into Wonder* in 1952. He believes that this unknown animal was wild, although it had been partially domesticated by the Lucayan Indians for food. "Dogs," he wrote, "they most certainly were not, and the best candidate seems to be the coati." It would seem they made gentle pets. And one could forgive the uncultured Spaniards if they thought them doglike. American pioneers, no better instructed, called the gopher a praire dog.

Orozco y Berra's studies of ancient Mexico resulted in the work entitled *Historia Antigua y de la Conquista de Mexico*. It was published in 1880, and in Book II he wrote,

The Aztecs had only three domesticated quadrupeds, all of which carried the root word "itzcuintli," which the Spaniards translated as "dog" because of the similarity of them with that animal.

The Aztecs appear to have quit breeding pets after the Conquest; meanwhile, the Spaniards ate all they could buy or catch. One of the quadrupeds, though very rare, can still be found in the wild. Called the tepeitzcuintli, it is the agouti.

The itzcuintlipotzoli may have been the guinea pig, or cavy. Others have suggested it might have been a variety of the Hutia. Whatever it was, it had a humped back, appeared to have no neck, and it had a rodent nose, that is, a Roman nose.

The third domesticated quadruped was the long-extinct Xoloitz-cuintli, or giant Quemi. Nearly hairless, it was reported to have been four feet long. It should not be confused with the modern Xoloitzcuintli, which is a true dog that also is nearly hairless.

Father Jose de Acosta* was a very learned man who was on the Council of the Indies. He left Spain in 1570 and spent fifteen years in the New World—in Santo Domingo, Peru, and Mexico. Admittedly, he arrived rather late, but he did interview some of the conquistadors who were still living. He said he also found it a good practice to question the Indians. If they did not have a word for an animal, but used the Spanish name, then

*Natural and Moral History of the Indies, translated from the Spanish by Edward Grimston, 1604.

he judged the Spaniards had brought it from Spain. As I have said, Alco is an Incan word, and below, Father Acosta is writing of the animals of Peru.

At the first there were no dogges at the Indies, but some beasts like unto little dogges, the which the Indians call Alco, and therefore they call all dogges that go from Spain by the same name, by reason of the resemblance that is betwixt them.

Father Acosta came to believe that either the story of Noah and the Ark was a lie, or God had made a second creation. For, he reasoned, the New World animals were not known in Europe, Africa, or Asia. And they could not have swum the Atlantic Ocean.

Amerigo Vespucci made a similar remark when he touched South America. Noah's Ark, he said, could not have held all the animals. Vespucci's voyages have been called fiction for centuries, but modern physicists and astronomers have proved from his records that he actually made the trips. He also is credited with developing the present system for computing longitude.

When a Spanish navigator named Vicente Yanez Piñzon reached the coast of Brazil early in January 1500, Spain did nothing to claim the discovery. For one thing, the Treaty of Tordesillas in 1494 had established that any lands found in the area which would become Brazil were to belong to Portugal. So it was Pedro Alvares Cabral who started out from Portugal with an armada and reached Brazil on April 22 the same year. He was to follow Vasco da Gama's recently discovered all-water route to the Spice Islands, that is, around the Cape of Good Hope.

Da Gama had made out Cabral's sailing orders. To avoid the disastrous calms of the Gulf of Guinea, as well as certain problems for the ships, Cabral was to sail far to the west. Da Gama's instructions would carry Cabral within two hundred miles of the coast of Brazil. He then would have known he was close to a land mass because of shore debris, land birds, and so on. He disobeyed instructions, sailed on, and claimed Brazil for Portugal. Cabral, like Vespucci, found no dogs in Brazil, but the Portuguese, as did the Spaniards, brought them. And they were not shepherd dogs, but war dogs.

On his later voyages, Columbus carefully detailed the number of his fighting men. He named the horses, told their colors, estimated their quality for riding and their steadiness in battle. He also gave in some detail "the most fearsome weapon of all"—the dogs. These "weapons" were taught to "bite out the bellies" of the Indians, and the Indians were virtually defenseless.* Usually called Bloodhounds, the dogs were, in fact, of Mastiff type. Their descendants can be seen today in the Fila Brasiliero, the national dog of Brazil, and in dogs sometimes seen in Venezuela. The following tale gives some idea of their savagery.

There is a hotel in Caracas called the Tamanaco. It is named after an Indian cacique (chief) who organized a rebellion against the Spaniards. When the Spaniards learned of the plot, they surprised and captured Tamanaco. A small stadium was erected, and other Indian caciques were invited to attend.

The best of the Spanish dogs, one named "Amigo," was starved for several days. Then Tamanaco was stripped and put into the stadium. Amigo attacked him, killed him, and tore off his head. The horrified Indians dropped their plot.

Colonel Joaquin Acosta wrote a book called *Compendio Historico del Descubrimiento y Colonizacion de la Nueva Granada.* Nueva Granada later became Colombia. In writing of the advance on Bogota, Colonel Acosta had this to say:

Although the tribes of those valleys put up some resistance, they were soon broken down and routed by the horses (cavalry), for they held them in such terror that one night when the Spaniards were encamped close to a little village, two or three horses that had got loose and galloped through the valley neighing and jumping, were sufficient to disperse the Indians who thought they were as ferocious as the Bloodhounds, and argued that if dogs made such havoc in their ranks, how much more terrible the larger animals must be.

Ponce de Leon had perhaps the most famous dog of its time—a Mastiff type war dog named Becerillo (little cow-calf). Balboa bought one of his pups, paying what was said to have been a very high price for it. Huge, yellowish brown, and ugly, the dog was named Leoncico (lion cub). Balboa won a lot of bets by proving that Leoncico could tell the difference between a good Indian and a bad one, and a Spaniard from both. The dog was so savage that he was said to be worth twenty men in battle; he drew a crossbowman's pay.

Historia de las Indias, by Bartolome de las Casas

174

On one occasion, Balboa was taking a siesta while some of his men were playing a game with dice. An aged woman came into camp, and Leoncico, who was seldom tied, immediately attacked her. He grabbed an arm, threw her to the ground, then held her there. The witness said the woman pleaded, "Sir dog, have mercy on me. I only came to beg for food and mercy for my people." Whereupon, Leoncico released the woman but then stood over her and urinated. The soldiers were shy of meat for their dogs and wanted to kill her. But Balboa refused, saying that if Leoncico had mercy on her, he could do no less.

Pedro de Cieza de Leon was a youth of fourteen when he came from Spain to join the conqueror Francisco Pizarro in Peru. He seems to have preferred writing to drunkenness and raping Inca women. In the *Travels of Pedro de Cieze de Leon, A.D. 1532-1550*, which were translated by Sir Clements R. Markham for the Hakluyt Society, he wrote,

> About the houses of the Indians many dogs are seen, which are very different from the Spanish kind, and about the size of ordinary curs: they call them Chonos.

The word is not in the Inca dictionary, and I have not been able to learn its meaning from natural history authorities in western South America. There is, however, an archipelago by that name in Chile.

Late in the last century, the Necropolis of Ancon in Peru* was opened. German archaeologists W. Reiss and A. Stubel sent artifacts to the Museum of Natural History in New York. Among them were the mummies of three dogs. At the same time, the museum had dog fossils from Colombia. None of these was dated, all being said only to be "before the conquest."

James Watson, an American all-breed dog judge and author of *The Dog Book* (1906), did investigate and study the remains. "Mummy No. 2," he wrote, "was so large as to force the question as to its being a dog." He concluded, however, that strange as it was, it was a dog. Another was very oddly marked. He stated further:

> Taking these relics as a whole, coupled with some fragmentary bone remains, we are safe in saying that there were no large dogs in that section of South America, but that they ranged from 12 to 18 inches in

---

The Necropolis of Ancon in Peru, 1875.

175

height, and varied in type from the square fronted, possibly undershot jaw, to the extreme of the Borzoi and fineness of the Italian Greyhound.

Alvar Nuñez, Cabeza de Vaca, was a lieutenant in the expedition of Pamphilo Narvaez, which left Spain in 1527. Narvaez was lost during a mighty storm in the Gulf of Mexico, but Cabeza de Vaca and three companions reached shore west of the Mississippi. They moved into the interior, then walked westward, whereupon they met Coronado moving north and eventually reached Mexico City.

Most of the Indian tribes that Cabeza de Vaca encountered were desperately poor. He mentions dogs only twice, but I am not certain whether the first reference is simply one of contempt or if it actually refers to dogs. Considering the poverty he describes, it seems unlikely that the tribes actually had dogs. In 1905, Fanny Bandelier translated the 1542 edition of Cabeza de Vaca's work, in which he wrote the following two passages.

It is the custom of theirs to kill even their own children for the sake of dreams, and the girls when newly born, they throw away to be eaten by dogs. They kill their own children and buy those of strangers.

. . . .

Their principle food are two kinds of roots, which they hunt for all over the land; they are unhealthy, inflating, and it takes two days to roast them . . . . But those people are so much exposed to starvation that these roots are to them indispensable, and they walk two and three leagues to get them. Now and then they kill deer, and at times get a fish, but there is so little and their hunger is so great that they eat spiders and ant eggs, worms, lizards, salamanders, and serpents, also vipers, the bite of which is deadly. They swallow earth and wood, and all they can get, the dung of deer, and things I do not mention . . . .

Cabeza de Vaca and his companions were passed from tribe to tribe, partly because they were considered to be medicine men who could cure diseases. One tribe apparently did have some dogs.

And we finally grew so hungry that we purchased two dogs, in exchange for nets and other things, and a hide with which I used to cover myself.

176

I made a contract with the Indians to make combs, arrows, bows, and nets for them. Also we made matting of which their lodges are constructed, and of which they are in very great need, for although they know how to make it, they do not like to do any work, in order to be able to go in quest of food; whenever they work they suffer greatly from hunger.

One of the most famous, or infamous, documents in the history of the Spanish conquests of North America is *Discovery and Conquest of Terra Florida by Don Hernando de Soto*. It was written by a "Gentleman of Elvas" and was translated out of the Spanish by Richard Hakluyt. The scene for the following quote, taken from the 1611 translation, is at Guaxule, somewhere near Rome, Tennessee.

The Indians there gave him a present of 300 dogges, because they saw the Christians esteeme them, and sought them to feed on them, for among them (the Indians) they are not eaten.

In his "Life of Father Marquette" (*American Biography*, Volume X), Jared Sparks comments on two accounts of de Soto's trip—the one by the Gentleman of Elvas and another by Garcilasco de la Vega. De la Vega was the son of an Incan princess and a Spanish nobleman who served Pizarro. He was taken to Spain while still a young man, so neither "the Inca," as he was known, nor the Gentleman of Elvas ever visited North America.

It may be doubted, at least, whether either of these works can be trusted as affording genuine historical materials. They have been cited by respectable writers in default of other authorities; but they border so closely upon the regions of romance, that they may as justly be ranked in this class of compositions, as in that of history. This is generally conceded in regard to Garcilasco. His predecessor, the Gentleman of Elvas, is thought to have higher claims, and perhaps he has, yet whoever follows him closely will be likely to run into 10 errors in arriving at a single truth, with the additional uncertainty of being unable to distinguish the former from the latter.

Even though de Soto and Cabeza de Vaca were in different parts of America, one must compare Cabeza de Vaca's account with that of the

Gentleman of Elvas. (Indeed! Three hundred dogs kept by a single tribe!) An 1887 issue of the *North American Review* comments on de Soto's trip. In reading the following quote, bear in mind that Spain had the finest international lawyers, was the dominant power in Europe at the time, and was quick to lay claim to the discoveries made by its explorers. Also, the explorers had promised the Spanish Crown heaps of gold in return for financing their trips. And some of the explorers were not finding any.

All this is a romantic and interesting tale; but for how large a portion of it we are indebted only to the vivid fancy of a Spanish historian, it is impossible to say; exaggerations and imaginative details may easily be detected in it by internal evidence. Spain made no attempt to take possession of the country to which this expedition, if real, had given it a valid claim, nor did any of its subjects venture to follow the track of de Soto's discoveries.

In 1929, in the old imperial palace of Istanbul, formerly Constantinople, a surprising discovery was made. This was a map painted on parchment, which was made by a Turkish admiral named Piri Ibn Haji Memmed. He is known generally as Piri Re'is. The map is dated 1513. In his notes, the admiral said that he based part of the map on one Columbus had had and upon which Columbus had sketched in the West Indies. This, of couse, set historians on a search for the long fabled map Columbus was said to have possessed. It has never been found.

Piri Re'is also wrote that he had used a map which once had belonged to Alexander the Great. He also wrote that he had used twenty-one earlier maps to make his. Columbus, himself, left one clue. In his journal for September 25, 1492, some three weeks before the discovery of land, he wrote,

The Admiral talked with Martin Alonzo Piñzon, Captain of the other caravel, the Pinta, concerning a chart which three days before he had sent to the caravel and in which, as it appears, the Admiral had certain islands depicted as being in that sea.

From Cabral's trip to Brazil there is a record of a letter he sent to the King of Portugal. In it, Cabral asks His Majesty to consult "an old map of the area." Again one has to ask, if Columbus had such a map, and if Cabral had one, then who made them, when, and where?

Now Piri Re'is drew his map in 1513. The startling thing is that Africa and South America are shown in correct longitude, although no mention of computing longitude was known by anyone of record until the invention of the chronometer, 250 years after Piri Re'is drew his map.

Moreover, the maps upon which Piri Re'is based his were made by cartographers who knew spherical trigonometry. This, too, was unknown until long after the era of the great European explorers. Finally, the ancient charts seem to show a part of Antarctica—Queen Maud's Land—before the Ice Age covered it. The maps seem to show that some of the sea bottom off Queen Maud's Land had been mapped also.

Charles H. Hapgood, professor of the History of Science at Keene State College of the University of New Hampshire, organized a study group to uncover the truth of the Piri Re'is map. He, his students, Naval Observatory scientists, and others spent almost a decade on the work.

They were forced to conclude that an advanced civilization had existed, possibly during the Ice Age. The people had known Antarctica when it was ice free and had known Europe toward the end of the last Ice Age. The maps also seem to indicate that there had been mighty land upheavals, and there is speculation that a continent may have sunk beneath the Atlantic.*

In 1983, Dr. Thomas Dillehay of the University of Kentucky and anthropologists from the Southern University of Chile began excavations at Monte Verde, eight hundred miles south of Santiago. There, planned row houses had once been built, and carbon dating of the remains dates them as ten thousand to fourteen thousand years old. Dr. Dillehay reported the discovery and excavation to the National Science Foundation early in 1984.

Some food remains also were discovered. Miraculously preserved because they had been covered by a clay or peatlike substance, the remains included potatoes and some fruits. This indicates that the people who built the planned row houses belonged to a culture sufficiently advanced to permit travel and to visit other people. For some of the food could not have been grown that far south.

Since the time of the Ancient Greeks, the story of Atlantis has intrigued geographers and historians. But there is an angle to all this that

*Hapgood, C. H. *Maps of the Ancient Sea Kings,* Dutton, 1979.

concerns the animals. Geographers and marine authorities generally agree that North and South America were once together, then were separated, then finally came together again in what is called Central America.

For a long time, naturalists have noted the great differences between the animals of North and South America. So did the first of the educated explorers to arrive in this hemisphere. This was partly explained by the jungles and mountains of Central America, which might have formed a barrier too difficult for most animals to cross. The separation of the two continents would increase the separate developments of the animals.

I believe the fossil record is too complete to doubt that there were domestic dogs in North America at the time of the Spanish conquest and exploration. The conclusions of the early educated Spaniards that there were no domestic dogs when they arrived must remain a puzzle.

I think it is certain that the Eskimos had dogs. At least those who settled the Arctic coastline and Greenland had them. We cannot know about the mysterious race that seems to have been there first.

By the time Captain George Vancouver explored the Pacific Northwest for England (1790-1795), domestic dogs were kept by most of the Indian tribes. They are described as having been dogs of no particular type and of no particular use except as pets.

But the situation in South America is still unsolved. There are some strange doglike mammals in this continent. If there was an early high culture that is now extinct, these doglike mammals may be canids that over thousands of years, have evolved along different lines. Some candidates come to mind. One is the now-extinct Falkland Islands wolf; another is the charming maned wolf. Neither appears to be a true wolf or true fox. A third candidate might be the bush dog.

Nonetheless, one conclusion cannot be doubted. All the known dog breeds in either North or South America result from importation from Europe, Asia, or Africa, including the Near East. Of course, some breeds have been developed from imported stocks—the Chesapeake Bay Retriever, Nova Scotia Duck Tolling Retriever, and the now-extinct Tahltan Bear Dog. The Xoloitzcuintli of Mexico is a possible exception.

Any breeds native to South America have long since disappeared to be replaced by modern breeds. Only the Mastiff type war dogs of the conquistadors, both Spanish and Portuguese, have left any impressions. The Fila Brasiliero of Brazil and a possibly extinct dog of similar type in Venezuela are exceptions.

21.   *Australia and the East Indies*

If the dog made its bond with man somewhere in Central Asia, they probably traveled together along the trade routes through India. One such route would go to Sri Lanka (Ceylon). Today Sri Lanka is the home of the Sinhala Hound. It has some of the features of a primitive dog, but it is a modern development insofar as efforts to stabilize it as a purebred are concerned.

Other ancient trade routes, or "migration routes," led into Malaysia; still others into New Guinea. There is a primitive dog in Malaysia, the Telomian, which is named after a river in the country. The Telomian is a true dog in every sense, although it maintains a few characteristics that must have been common in the earliest dogs. Some Telomians have been brought to the United States, both for study and as family pets.

How and when the Dingo arrived in Australia is still a puzzle. But a variety of the Dingo is named the New Guinea Dingo, and many Australian animals seem to have arrived from New Guinea. This suggests that a land bridge once must have existed between the continent and New Guinea.

Fossil Dingo remains have been found in close association with those of Thylacoleo, the Marsupial Lion; Polarchestes, the giant kangaroo; and the hippopotamus-like Euryzgoma. No fossil human bones have been found in association with these.

Another migration route might have been by way of Melville and the Coburg Peninsula, a most inhospitable area. It is possible that an earlier people than the Aborigines followed this route into Australia, bringing with them their Dingo dogs. However, they found the environment so difficult that they decided to return to their homelands.

Perhaps they took some of their dogs on the return, but perhaps many were left behind. The dogs multiplied, then radiated out over the entire continent. They were there when the present Australoids, or Aborigines, arrived to compete with them for food.

William Dampier, an English buccaneer, navigator, and hydrographer, was also a writer. His reports on his voyages made him world famous, and although untrained, he had a surprisingly accurate knowledge of natural history.

In Dampier's day, Australia was known as New Holland. It had been so named to honor Abel Janszoon Tasman, the greatest of the Dutch navigators and certainly one of the greatest of all time. He had circumnavigated Australia, and the Tasman Sea and Tasmania are still named for him. Tasman never reported seeing dogs. But Jan Carstensz, another Dutch explorer-navigator, reported seeing the tracks of men and large dogs.

Dampier made one report in 1688; he made a further report the next year, which was published in 1703. This is the earliest information on the Dingo, and it indicates how difficult life was for the people and their dogs, at least in that part of Australia. The work also lends some support to the theory that the Dingoes were left behind by an earlier people who decided to desert Australia. A small excerpt follows.

There are but few Land Animals. I saw some lizards, and my men saw two or three Beasts like hungry wolves, lean like so many skeletons, being nothing but skin and bones. Tis probable that it was the Foot on one of those Beasts that I mentioned as seen by us in New Holland.

The Dingo is a true dog. It shares certain characteristics with other primitive dogs such as the Basenji. It does not bark, but neither is it mute. Both sexes seem to have a heat period only once each year. The Dingo has twenty-four-hour eyes; that is, it can see quite well at night, but does not suffer from bright daylight. Also it is a feral dog.

One definition of feral is "having escaped from domestication and become wild." But feral animals, even when living in the wild and "off the land," still remember that they are domestic animals, bonded to people. Therefore, they easily return to domestication. The wild horses of the American West are a perfect example of this.

The Dingo appears in the background of two of Australia's purebred dogs—the Stumpy-tailed Cattle Dog, and the Australian Cattle Dog, or Blue Heeler. Starting about 1830 a cattle drover named Timmins began crossing Dingoes into his drovers' dogs.

The problem for drovers was that cattle had to be driven for long distances to the marketplaces, sometimes taking as long as a week. The native dogs were terrible barkers, and this upset the cattle. But since Dingoes don't bark, Timmins decided to crossbreed. Dingoes also like to attack their prey from the rear. Timmins' crossbreds were enthusiastic drovers, but they liked to bite the heels of the cattle. So they became known as Timmins Biters. However, with careful breeding, the dogs were brought under reasonable restraint.

When Europeans first began to settle in Australia, there were two varieties of Dingo. The highland Dingo was somewhat larger than its cousin of the deserts and plains. It seems probable that food was more plentiful, so that after centuries of life in the highlands the highland Dingoes just grew larger. A modern example can be cited of dogs of various breeds which, when brought to America and placed upon our modern dog foods, have grown larger.

The highland type is now very rare. But in fact, both varieties are becoming so. Stock breeders have killed vast numbers of them. Even in areas where they still appear to be plentiful, purebred Dingoes are becoming rare. The reason is that thousands of European dogs run wild, and Dingoes readily mate with them. This has been particularly true near campsites.

Dingoes return to domesticity quite readily, but especially if taken into the home as pups. However, they are like the Telomians. They have been accustomed to wild freedom too long. They do not like to be tied up or penned up. If allowed to be loose, they wander. Most cannot be trusted about chickens.

Australia's modern dogs are now well known in the rest of the world. They have been developed by crossing with English breeds. These are the Australian Terrier, and the Silky Terrier. The dog known in the United States as the Australian Shepherd Dog has no provable link to Australia. Its ancestry could include the Border Collie, and it is a herding dog of excellent quality.

183

Relief at the end of a balustrade. Iran, Mongol Period, about 1304. Courtesy The Cleveland Museum of Art. Purchase from the H. J. Wade Fund.

War dog, possibly Hecate's, attacks a giant in frieze around ruined Altar of Zeus at Pergamon, near Smyrna, in Asia Minor. Constructed about 160 B.C., the altar and its frieze are considered the finest monument to Hellenistic art. Courtesy State Museum of Berlin.

184

22.   *Asia in General*

And the Lord God planted a garden in Eden, in the East. And there he
put man whom he had formed. (Gen. 2:8)

Until quite recently, the birthplace of Man has been believed to have
been in either Asia Minor or central Asia. The Bible places the Garden of
Eden in Asia Minor, along the Euphrates River, but all attempts to locate
its site have failed. The Sumerians said they came "from the East," and
the people who built the city of Mohenjo Daro, as well as others who built
along the Indus River Valley, probably also arrived from the East.

Today, many paleoanthropologists place the origin of the human race
in Africa. But Asia is still greatly attractive as the origin of the domestic
dog family. The oldest dog fossil ever found was located in Pelagawra,
Iraq. And the great hordes of warrior tribes that burst from Asia into
Europe, Asia Minor, and North Africa had dogs, often fantastic numbers
of them—war dogs, hunting dogs, flock guardians, flock herders, even
pet dogs.

Asia is a huge land mass, with high mountains separating fertile
valleys. Such valleys were ideal for developing dog breeds. Their
comparative isolation and highland stock grazing areas challenged the
people within to produce dogs for specialized purposes. And the
plasticity of canine germ plasm, with its huge gene pool, made it possible
to develop specialized breeds in a very short time.

Asia also has many deserts, which required different kinds of dogs.
From these regions would come the coursing dogs—animals that could
serve in the chase. Heavily forested areas, on the other hand, demanded
other types of dogs, as did the lands above the tree line and in the Arctic.

Several Alpine passes permitted migration into Europe. From Tibet,
migrants could travel through the mountains and go down the Indus
River Valley to Hyderabad, Karachi, and Rawalpindi. Or they could go
northeastward to Mongolia, China, and Japan.

Others could take the Ganges River into a different part of India and cross over into Ceylon (Sri Lanka). Some would reach the sea at Bombay. And many would live in or on the outskirts of the great Indian deserts—the area that may account for such cursorial hounds as the Afghan, Persian Greyhound, Mahratta, and others.

A few migrants would cross over the sea, perhaps hop-skipping by way of modern Bahrain. They would travel to ancient Sumeria, then either skirt or pass through the desert at Iraq, and go around or through the mountains to Baghdad and Al Basra. Others would push on, skirting the deserts around the Persian Gulf at Abadan and Basra to reach Egypt, where cursorial hounds such as the Saluki may have been developed.

Not all the migrants—the warriors, their tribes, and nomad followers—would take the mountain passes to the south or even into southern Europe. Some would push, or be pushed, north into Russia and Siberia. Here other dog breeds would be developed, some for hauling sledges, others for hunting in the forest. Migrants also would move into Turkey, and some would settle in the Balkans. Then, faced with the menace of wolves, jackals, and hyenas, they would develop the great flock guardians—the Anatolian, Karabash, Ovcharkas, Outcharkas, Komondor, Kuvasz, Jugoslavian Shar Planinetz, Italian Maremma, and Great Pyrenees.

Asia is such a vast continent that not all dogs would push west, south, and north with warrior or nomadic tribes. Tibetans would develop both guard and pet dogs. They would travel the trade routes into China and Mongolia, taking dogs to trade as well as to guard their caravans.

If the theory of cultural centers is an accurate explanation of how the world became populated, then most primitive people should be found at the ends of the earth, like the Patagonians at the tip of South America and the Aborigines in Australia. Similarly, if the theory is applied to dogs, then the most primitive of these should also be found at the ends of the earth, or at least in very isolated areas. Indeed, having once migrated with their human masters, the Basenji is now found in the jungles in Africa, the Dingo in Australia, the Sinhala in Sri Lanka, and the Pelomian in New Guinea.

I believe that the domestic dog was born in central Asia. I am not willing, however, to concede that it developed from a small Chinese wolf, nor from four now-extinct wolf varieties. Instead, I believe that both wolf and dog developed from an unknown Pleistocene canid that lived some sixty thousand years ago. The two animals differed psychologically:

the wolf was a wild animal, the dog possessed an urge toward domestication.

From as early as the time of Aristotle, naturalists have recognized that some form of evolution has taken place. Darwin based part of his work on the natural selection theory developed by Alfred Russel Wallace. Considered the father of zoogeography, Wallace was a contemporary of Darwin. In his *Arawak Law* and *Ternate Paper,* Wallace proposed the process of divergence.

Wallace believed that all living things had a tendency to diverge. Thus, slightly different forms would appear even while the parent form existed. Those that were not an improvement over the parent form would not survive. Those that were would prosper and eventually would produce further divergencies.

Now the wolf has been around for a long time—at least 60,000 years, if I am correct. Modern wolf families do not differ from extinct species to a significant degree. And the differences among contemporary wolf families are comparatively minor. Even skilled authorities will disagree on their classifications.

The family of the domestic dog, however, shows astonishing divergencies. In fact, more than four hundred dog breeds are estimated to exist. Most of their differences are physical, but there are mental differences as well. And few could survive in the wild today except primitive forms such as the Dingo.

The evidence indicates to me that the dog has had an amazing ability to diverge, even though the divergencies have been and are induced by man's breeding policies and whims. Thus I conclude that, like Wallace's simile of the tree, from one limb of the Canidae tree came two divergent animals—the wolf and the dog.

Bibliography

Alciphron. *Letters from the Country and the Town, Of Fishermen, Farmers, Parasites, and Courtesans.* Translated by F. A. Wright. Broadway Translations, 1923.

Arrian. *The Campaigns of Alexander.* Translated by Aubrey de Selincourt. Middlesex, England: Penguin, 1981.

Ash, Edward C. *Dogs: Their History & Development.* 2 vols. London: Ernest Benn, 1927.

Bernstrom, John. *Herre Ock Hund.* N.p.: Svenska Kennelklubben, 1964.

Bower, Capt. H. *Diary of a Journey Across Tibet.* Calcutta, 1893.

Brilliant, Richard. *Pompeii—AD 79.* New York: Clarkson N. Potter, 1979.

Brinton, Daniel G. *The Myths of the New World.* Philadelphia: McKay, 1896.

Caldwell, Elsie Noble. *Alaska Trail Dogs.* Richard R. Smith, 1945.

Chadwick, John. *The Mycenaean World.* Cambridge: Cambridge University Press, 1976.

Clark, Kenneth. *Animals and Men.* New York: William Morrow, 1977.

Collier, V. W. F. *Dogs of China and Japan in Nature and Art.* New York: Frederick A. Stokes (1923).

Coon, Carleton S. *The Seven Caves.* New York: Knopf, 1957.

Craven, Thomas. *The Pocket Book of Greek Art.* New York: Pocket, 1950.

Cristofani, Mauro. *The Etruscans: A New Investigation.* New York: Galahad, 1979.

Cunliffe, Barry. *The Celtic World.* New York: McGraw, 1979.

Dangerfield, Stanley, and Elsworth Howell, eds. *The International Encyclopedia of Dogs.* New York: Howell, 1974.

Dogs of Australia: Melbourne: Humphrey & Formula, n.d.

do Valle, Procopio. *O Grande Livro Do Fila Brasileiro.* Rio de Janeiro: Nobel, 1981.

Duncan, David Douglas. *Great Treasures of the Kremlin.* New York: Crown, 1979.

Duplaix, Nicole, and Noel Simon. *World Guide to Mammals.* New York: Crown, 1976.

Fiennes, Richard. *The Order of Wolves.* Bobbs-Merrill, 1976.

Fiennes, Richard and Alice. *The Natural History of Dogs.* American Museum of Natural History, 1970.

FitzGerald, Patrick. *Ancient China: The Making of the Past.* Oxford: Elsevier, 1978.

Fol, Alexander, and Ivan Marazov. *Thrace & the Thracians.* New York: St. Martin, 1977.

Grenard, F. *Tibet: The Country and Its Inhabitants.* Translated by A. Texeira de Mattos. London, 1904.

Hadingham, Evan. *Secrets of the Ice Age*. New York: Walker, 1979.

Hamilton-Wilkes, Monty, and David Cumming. *Kelpie and Cattle Dog: The Australian Dogs and Work*. Sydney: Angus and Robertson, 1967.

Hawkes Jacquetta. *The Atlas of Early Man*. New York: St. Martin, 1976.

———. ed. *The World of the Past*. Vol 1. New York: Simon and Schuster, 1963.

Holdich, T. Hungerford. *Tibet the Mysterious*. N.p., n.d.

Hull, Denison Bingham. *Hounds and Hunting in Ancient Greece*. Chicago: University of Chicago Press, 1964.

Kuhn, Herbert. *The Rock Pictures of Europe*. New York: October, 1956.

The Last Two Million Years. Pleasantville, N.Y.: Reader's Digest, 1977.

Leach, Maria. *God Had a Dog*. Rahway, N.J.: Rutgers University Press, 1961.

Lopez de Gomara, Francisco. *The Conquest of the West India*. N.p. Readex Microprint, 1966.

MacQueen, James. *Babylon*. New York: Frederick Praeger, 1965.

Markham, Sir C. R. *Narratives of the Mission of George Bogle to Tibet*. (The Journey of Thomas Manning to Lhasa, 1879). N.p., n.d.

Mech, L. David. *The Wolf, American Museum of Natural History*. 1970.

Mellaart, James. *The Archaeology of Ancient Turkey*. Totowa, New Jersey: Rowman, 1978.

Moore, Daphne. *Foxhounds*. North Pomfret, Vermont: Batsford, 1981.

Olsen, Stanley J., John W., and Qi Guo Qin. "The Position of *Canis lupus vaiabilis*, From Zhoukoudian, In the Ancestral Lineage of the Domestic Dog, *Canis familiaris*. N.p., n.d. Mimeograph.

Phillips, Carleton J., Raymond P. Coppinger, and David S. Schimel. *Hyperthermia in Running Sled Dogs*. Hempstead, New York: N.p., 1981. Pamphlet.

Riddle, Maxwell. *Lovable Mongrel*. Fon du Lac, Wisconsin: All-Pets Books, 1954.

———. *This is the Chihuahua*. Jersey City, N.J.: T.F.H., 1959.

———. *The Wild Dogs in Life and Legend*. New York: Howell, 1979.

Sabella, Frank, and Shirlee A. Kalstone. *The Art of Handling Show Dogs*. Hollywood, California: B & E, 1980.

Salisbury, Charlotte Y. *Tibetan Diary, and Travels Along the Old Silk Route*. New York: Walker, 1981.

Sanderson, Ivan T. *Living Mammals of the World*. Doubleday, 1967.

Sauter, Marc-R. *Switzerland, From Earliest Times to the Roman Conquest*. Boulder, Colorado: Westview, 1976.

Smythe, R. H. *The Conformation of the Dog*. London: Popular Dogs, 1957.

Specht, Robert. *Tisha*. New York: St. Martin's Press, 1976.

The Splendors of Dresden. New York: Newsweek, 1979.

Stapleton, Michael. *A Dictionary of Greek and Roman Mythology*. New York: Bell, 1978.

Swedrup, Ivan, Erik O. Stovling, and Kris Sandberg. *Hunter I Bild*. Stockholm: N.p., 1980.

Thomas, Joseph B. *Hounds and Hunting Through the Ages*. New York: Windward House, 1933.

Vlahos, Olivia. *Far Eastern Beginnings*. New York: Viking, 1976.

Walker, Gen. J. T. *Four Years Journeyings through Great Tibet*. Proceedings of the Royal Geographic Society, Vol. 7. 1885.

Watson, James. *The Dog Book*. Vol. 1. New York: Doubleday, 1906.

Index

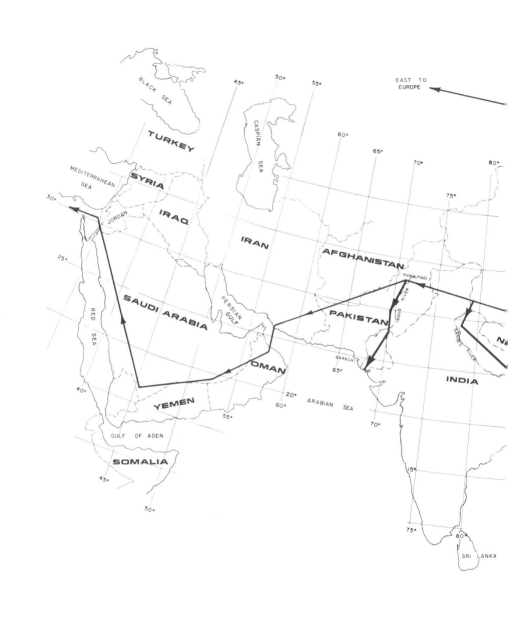